## PRAISE FOR

# THE 37TH PARALLEL

"Fascinating. . . . Chuck Zukowski takes up UFO investigations as a hobby, but it slowly turns into something more. . . . Mezrich approaches the material seriously, preserving the human element but taking care to present the facts. Zukowski's realization that many sightings and events line up along the 37th parallel is the culmination of years of investigations, and after thrilling stories of lights in the sky, screams in the night, and mysterious dark helicopters, readers will be more than ready for the exciting revelation."

—*Publishers Weekly*

"Mezrich writes vividly and grippingly. . . . It all makes a terrific story."

—*Washington Post*

"[E]xtremely engaging. . . . The inclusion of photos and important documents really helps the reader understand the intricacies of the investigation."

—Press Association (UK)

# THE 37TH PARALLEL

## THE SECRET TRUTH BEHIND
## AMERICA'S UFO HIGHWAY

# BEN MEZRICH

**ATRIA** PAPERBACK

New York   London   Toronto   Sydney   New Delhi

**ATRIA**
PAPERBACK

An Imprint of Simon & Schuster, Inc.
1230 Avenue of the Americas
New York, NY 10020

First Atria Paperback edition June 2017

**ATRIA** PAPERBACK and colophon are trademarks of Simon & Schuster, Inc.

For information about special discounts for bulk purchases,
please contact Simon & Schuster Special Sales at 1-866-506-1949
or business@simonandschuster.com.

The Simon & Schuster Speakers Bureau can bring authors to your
live event. For more information, or to book an event, contact the
Simon & Schuster Speakers Bureau at 1-866-248-3049 or visit our
website at www.simonspeakers.com.

Interior design by Dana Sloan

Manufactured in the United States of America

10  9  8  7  6  5

Library of Congress Cataloging-in-Publication Data

Names: Mezrich, Ben, 1969– author.
Title: The 37th parallel : the secret truth behind America's UFO highway /
   Ben Mezrich.
Other titles: Thirty-seventh parallel
Description: First Atria Books hardcover edition. | New York : Atria Books, 2016.
Identifiers: LCCN 2016021639 (print) | LCCN 2016032716 (ebook)
Subjects: LCSH: Unidentified flying objects—Southwestern States. |
   Parapsychology—Southwestern States. | BISAC: BODY, MIND & SPIRIT /
   Unexplained Phenomena. | BIOGRAPHY & AUTOBIOGRAPHY /
   Science & Technology. | BODY, MIND & SPIRIT / UFOs & Extraterrestrials.
Classification: LCC TL789.5.S85 M49 2016 (print) | LCC TL789.5.S85 (ebook) |
   DDC 001.9420979—dc23
LC record available at https://lccn.loc.gov/2016021639

ISBN 978-1-5011-3552-1
ISBN 978-1-5011-3553-8 (pbk)
ISBN 978-1-5011-3554-5 (ebook)

*To Asher and Arya, who are young enough to believe in little green men.*

*And to Tonya—after reading this you'll see that they aren't that little, and are probably gray.*

A generation from now, people will look back at us the same way we look back at those who believed the Earth was flat; the evidence that we've been visited by extraterrestrials is so overwhelming, it's actually a leap of faith to believe anything else.

*—Anonymous aerospace executive*

There's more physical evidence that UFOs exist than there's physical evidence that Jesus Christ existed.

*—Chuck Zukowski,*
*to the* Denver Post, *July 22, 2007*

# THE 37TH PARALLEL

# CHAPTER 1

37.2841° N, 108.7787° W

September 12, 2000. A stretch of interstate highway winding along the baseoftheUteMountainRangeneartheColorado–NewMexicoborder,a little after 4:00 p.m.

In a panoramic splash of pine trees and puffs of falling snow, flashes of brilliant sunlight reflected off the cap of Ute Peak, the Sleeping Mountain, high above. And then a beat-up RV lumbered into view. Over the rumble of the camper's engines rose the off-key tenor of an all-American family sing-along.

Chuck Zukowski was at the wheel of the twenty-four-foot Winnebago Warrior Class A, both hands tapping out the rhythm of "Sweet Home Alabama" on the thick vinyl of the steering wheel cover. Early forties, sandy-haired, fit, Chuck was smiling as he navigated the camper down the serpentine asphalt. His three kids were in the back, one girl and two boys, and his wife, Tammy, a pretty brunette, was up front, joining Chuck in keeping the beat with her fingers against the dash. From the lines beneath Chuck's blue eyes, it was obvious that they'd been driving for quite some time, but there was enough vivid scenery flashing by outside to keep even the youngest kid from getting bored. This sort of road trip was something the Zukowski clan enjoyed. In fact, when Chuck finally spotted the small ranch-style motel along the highway, coinciding with the notice from the dulcet tone of the RV's audio GPS, he was almost reluctant to pull in for the night.

After parking the RV in the empty motel lot, Chuck grabbed a pair of room keys from the lobby manager, and the Zukowski family settled into two adjoining rooms overlooking a tarp-covered pool. The kids went straight for the TV in their room, after a quick dinner, microwaved to perfection in the RV, but next door, Tammy headed for the bed and sank into it with a tattered paperback, exhausted from the long day in the camper.

A few hours later, the kids finally let the TV get some rest, and Chuck closed the door between the two rooms. The sun was long gone outside, the view of the shuttered pool replaced by an inky blackness, broken only by the occasional flare of neon from the vacancy sign hanging above the motel lobby. Tammy was still digging into the paperback, but Chuck could tell she was down for the night. He ran his fingers through her hair and then told her he was going out for a short walk. Barely looking up from the book, she asked him to get some ice from the machine on his way back.

He took the ice bucket from the mantel by the door and headed out to the parking lot. Opening the back of the RV, he leaned into a four-by-four storage compartment and reached toward a locked strongbox affixed to one wall. With a jangle of keys, he pried open the box and exchanged the ice bucket—which he would fill when he returned to the Winnebago—for his equipment: a three-pound police flashlight, a video recorder, an EMF counter, and three rectangular batteries. Then he reached for the leather holster hanging from a hook at the back of the box and removed his .40 caliber Glock from it before checking the cartridges and strapping it to his waist.

By the time he exited the RV, snow had started to fall again, but even so he could see the headlights snaking toward him down the desolate highway.

. . .

Two hours later Chuck was breathing hard as he burst through the last line of thick pines into a clearing following his two companions—an athletic man, midthirties, sporting a pony tail and dressed in a thick hunting jacket with a machete slung over one shoulder, and a thin, slightly older woman struggling along in a bulky snowsuit and too many scarves. Tufts of low grass covered in snow punctuated the field of icy gravel. The three of them were now at least eight thousand feet up, high enough to feel the altitude; the other man, Joe Fex, part Native American, a rugged outdoorsman reared on the ranches that pockmarked this corner of the country, was barely sweating as he began setting up their makeshift campsite, raising a canvas tent to protect their equipment. But the woman was trembling from exhaustion and certainly fear. Chuck had no worries about Fex; the big man was an old friend and had accompanied Chuck on many similar excursions over the years. But the woman was a wild card; Chuck had met her over the Internet not two weeks earlier, and the drive over to the base of this hike was the longest time Chuck had spent with her in person. Chuck would have been much happier if they could have left her behind—but it was her information that had brought them to this spot.

According to her website, she was supposed to be some sort of psychic. Chuck wasn't the type to judge anyone—for all he knew she had a cemetery full of dead people on speed dial. More likely, she was batshit crazy, but it didn't really matter. As usual, Chuck had done his research. The psychic might have been the first to turn him on to this particular location, but now he had a case file an inch thick on this place.

Case file or no, the next two hours licked past in near silence, the three of them getting colder as the wind picked up, rustling through the nearby pines and sending ice chips and gravel skittering across the ground. Chuck wondered if they should cut out and chalk it up as another in a long list of wild-goose chases. In a few more hours, the kids would be waking up, and Tammy would want to get back on the road and find someplace for a good, cheap breakfast. Maybe there was a Denny's somewhere up the interstate.

Chuck froze midthought, as he noticed something strange. The wind seemed to have stopped—not gradually, but suddenly—and the air went silent. He opened his mouth to say something to Joe, but before he could get the words out, there was a sudden flash of light in the pitch-black sky above. *Incredibly bright, at least three hundred feet up—and it stayed lit.* Before Chuck could shout for Joe to grab the camera from the tent, a second light joined the first, and the two flashes sprinted through the air in a wide arc. Then, it seemed as if the entire sky had opened up, lights exploding everywhere, brighter than the Fourth of July.

"Holy shit!" Chuck screamed. "Joe . . ."

Joe was already dashing at full speed around the psychic—who had curled into a ball on the ground, her face a mask of pure terror—and into the tent. He quickly returned with the camera and all three batteries. Chuck grabbed the camera from Joe's shaking hands, turned it toward the sky, hit the button—and . . . nothing.

The camera was dead.

Chuck cursed, yanking the battery out of the device, jamming the second fresh battery into the base. He hit the button again. And again, nothing. He tried the third battery, but it was obvious all three batteries were now, inexplicably, completely drained. Chuck felt his pulse rocketing in his veins. To have one backup battery go out would have been unusual—but all three?

"What the hell are they?" Joe shouted, as the two men stared at the lights arcing back and forth through the sky above them. "Helicopters?"

Chuck shook his head. His mouth was dry, his chest constricted with fear. He'd never seen anything like this before.

"No way. Helicopters can't move like that. Or fly that close together."

"A meteor shower? Some sort of discharge? Or . . ."

And just as suddenly as they had started, the lights vanished. Completely. The sky went back to black. A strange, intense silence spread across the clearing, severe as a leather belt snapping tight. Not a single tree branch twitched.

And then a high-pitched scream pierced the air, from somewhere below the tree line, maybe two hundred feet down the mountain.

*Christ.* Chuck looked at Joe as the screaming grew louder. There was a crashing of tree branches: Whatever was making that noise was coming toward them. *Some sort of animal, maybe an elk or a moose, running at full speed, screaming that unnerving, terrified scream.* Bearing down on them, louder and louder, diving headlong through the pines toward the clearing . . .

And then just as suddenly as it had started, the noise cut off dead, midscream. The animal, whatever it was, had been running from something. *Something that had taken it down in a single stroke.*

The breeze picked back up, and the night switched back to normal, as if none of what Chuck and his companions had just experienced had ever happened.

Chuck stared at Joe, at the way the big man was shivering beneath his hunting jacket, and then at the psychic, who was sobbing on the ground. Then he looked down at his own trembling hands, one of which was resting on the hilt of his .40, still in its holster.

He shook his head, completely unnerved.

"Whatever ran that animal down—this Glock isn't near big enough, is it?"

At that, even in his terrified state, he almost cracked a smile.

# CHAPTER 2

38.845858° N, 104.092197° W

Even after twenty years, the feeling of excitement still took Chuck by surprise, the intense burst of adrenaline that seemed to hijack his entire system the moment before he arrived at an incident site, the sense of anticipation that built in his chest, shortening his breath. Today, the long drive over from his home in Colorado Springs hadn't helped. Two hours was a lot of time to be alone with one's thoughts going through nothing but high, barren desert, broken by sporadic areas of low brush, dried-up streambeds, and the occasional barn.

When he finally reached the dirt turnoff to the fifty-acre cattle-and-horse ranch, whose owner, Glenda, had called him, he drove up and parked his pickup truck next to the house. He caught a glimpse of the rancher's face as she crossed the short distance from the edge of the grazing area where she'd been waiting for him. From both personal experience and his years on the force, he knew what fear looked like. Chuck had always been good at reading people—even before his training at the police academy in Colorado Springs, and the eight years since that he'd spent as a reserve sheriff's deputy in El Paso County. Anyone who'd been involved in law enforcement as long as he had had seen more than his fair share of terrified people. He'd been a first responder at scenes of domestic abuse, pulled people from burning cars and buildings, even helped cordon off shocked witnesses at the scorched debris field of a small plane crash. But the look on the rancher's face was something else, a shade of fear that Chuck was uniquely qualified to recognize, because he was one of a handful of people, in law enforcement and other fields, who'd seen it before.

"Morning," Glenda managed to say as she reached Chuck's truck. He had the door open, but was still sitting and gathering his equipment from the front passenger seat. Rubber gloves, plastic bags for samples, two cameras, his handheld electromagnetic field reader, and his gun. He was pretty certain the gun was unnecessary. If history was any predictor, whatever had hit this ranch several days earlier had come in fast and had finished just as suddenly.

"Made it as quickly as I could, ma'am," Chuck said as he got out and strapped the equipment to the special vest he wore. He'd designed it over the years, after responding to so many of these calls and learning what he would need for most of them. He placed the plastic bags and gloves into Velcro pouches along his ribs and the EMF reader and gun into holsters on either side. "I only wish I could have gotten here closer to when it happened."

Half a week since the incident—a truly frustrating lapse of time, but it couldn't be helped.

"I'm just glad you're here. The officers who came by the morning it went down were—well, less than useful."

Chuck could hear the distaste in her voice, and he completely understood. He'd already read the police report made by the two investigating officers who had stopped by the ranch after Glenda had first called 911. It was obvious the two cops had been far out of their comfort zone—Chuck couldn't really blame them for that. It was equally obvious that the officers hadn't been able to give the woman any comfort. It took a lot to traumatize a third-generation rancher, but a pair of cops from the El Paso County sheriff's department weren't going to be able to make much sense out of something like this.

Unlike the police officers, Chuck wasn't there in an official capacity. Although he had holstered his service revolver to his vest, and his badge was in the glove compartment of the truck, he wasn't wearing his uniform, and he wouldn't be filing any paperwork in Colorado Springs. In fact, he hadn't been alerted to the incident by anyone involved with the department, but by a television reporter whom he had worked with before, an on-air producer named Andy Koen who had put him in touch with Glenda. The fact that she'd even taken his call, and had immediately asked him to come down to her ranch, was a testament to how terrified she truly was. Ranchers weren't exactly known for welcoming outsiders; Chuck only hoped he could provide a little more explanation, if not consolation, than the investigating officers had.

They started away from the truck and into the ranch proper, Glenda moving determinedly past a low fence that marked the edge of the cows' free grazing area, Chuck a few feet behind. Immediately, Chuck could tell that something was off. He'd been on plenty of ranches over the years, and on the surface, Glenda's compound wasn't unusual. Eighty or so acres, twenty-five head of cattle, with a low house beyond the grazing area and a medium-sized barn attached to the horse corral directly ahead. But the farther they got from the road, the harder Chuck's heart started to beat. The low grass they were now moving through seemed untouched—*ungrazed*—and it was instantly obvious why that was. The handful of cows Chuck could see were clustered together in a small section of their feed area, as close to the barn as they could go. Beyond them, within the horse corral, the horses were behaving similarly—crowded together near the back fence. In the distance, he could hear a dog making noise from somewhere inside the house—a high-pitched sound, more wail than bark.

"They've been like that since it happened," Glenda said. "Huddled over there, by the barn." And then, almost as an afterthought: "They won't go near the bodies."

"On the phone, you said that at least one of the horses was nearby when it happened?"

Glenda nodded. "A survivor. A witness. Whatever you want to call him."

This was part of the reason for Chuck's elevated adrenaline level, beyond being at the site of the incident itself. It was extremely unusual for there to be any "survivors." Usually, there were only bodies.

"Over here."

Glenda led him the last few yards to the edge of the corral, where she unlatched a wooden gate and headed for the horses grouped together by the back. It took almost ten minutes for her to coax the animal away from the group; another ten for Chuck to get the poor thing comfortable enough with him so that he could approach.

It was a young male, a little over two years old, and to describe the animal as agitated would be a laughable understatement. He pawed at the ground, eyes rapidly shifting, spittle pooling at the edges of his mouth. Moving closer, Chuck immediately saw a reddish mark on the horse's upper nose—what looked to be some sort of cut, scrape, or even burn— about the size of a quarter. Following Glenda's lead, he bent low and saw similar marks on the inside of the animal's legs.

"And his behavior—the way he's acting—this is unusual for him?"

"Unusual? He's one of my husband's favorites. Like a pet. Him, Princess, and Buck, the three of them were inseparable."

Chuck nodded. Horses are different from other animals on a ranch— they're high maintenance, but more than that, they are often part of the family. Glenda and her husband—who, over the past few months, had grown too ill to tend to the ranch, leaving it under her watch—had raised these animals from foals. Beyond the emotional value, horses were expensive. Ranchers like Glenda ran their businesses at very tight margins. The unexpected loss of even a single animal hurt—losing multiple animals could mean the difference between a good season and a bad one.

"I don't know what I'm going to do with him. And the dog—she's even worse. Same sort of marks on her. Shaking, drooling, whining. She won't even come out of the house anymore."

From the corral, Chuck could still hear the dog's high-pitched wail. Nearly a week had gone by and the animal was still obviously traumatized. Chuck would want to take a closer look at the poor thing and run some tests on the agitated horse. But first, it was time to see the bodies. Without another word, Glenda led him toward the pasture where the incident had taken place.

Even from a distance, Chuck could tell that the two fully mature horses—Princess and Buck—lying prone in the grass had died unnaturally. The carcasses were flat against the ground on their sides, splayed out in exactly the same position. As Chuck drew closer, he could see no signs of predators or of any sort of defensive resistance—no deep hoofprints or raised furrows. They had obviously died suddenly. According to Glenda, they had been young, healthy animals, worth around a thousand dollars each.

Both horses had been stripped to the bone in various places. Much of their hides was still present, but the wounds were prolific, from head to haunch.

"You seen this sort of thing before?" Glenda asked, her voice low as they both stopped a few paces from the bodies.

Chuck pulled his rubber gloves out from the pouch on his vest and moved the last few feet to the closest corpse. His heart was pounding so hard it was difficult to keep his hands from shaking.

Yes, over the past decade, he'd seen this many times.

Even more terrifying, incidents like this had been going on for more than fifty years—this exact same scene had been witnessed and documented on ranches all over Colorado—as well as in New Mexico, Arizona, Utah, and many other places—decade after decade.

What had occurred on Glenda's ranch—as violent and horrifying as it was—was part of a phenomenon made up of more than ten thousand individual incidents, in a half dozen states—all of them completely unexplained.

*Ten thousand incidents.*

For the past ten years, Chuck had been pursuing the truth behind these kills and what he believed to be a connected but also unexplained phenomenon. This was his hobby, his obsession, his addiction . . .

"The wounds," Glenda whispered. "They look, well—surgical."

Chuck didn't respond. But as he peered closer, he could see that she was right. On both animals, the eyes had been carefully removed. Other wounds on what was left of the carcasses were precise, small, and yes, seemingly surgical—where internal organs had been excised. And the tongues had both been taken—cleanly, via perfectly straight incisions, far back in the throat.

And that wasn't even the worst part.

# CHAPTER 3

## ANZA, CALIFORNIA, LATE SPRING 1994

A little past 2:00 a.m., a perfect, cloudless night.

Sand, gravel, and bits of pavement fountained up from beneath the wheels of Chuck's Honda XL 250 as he took the last hairpin curve as fast as he dared, his left knee so close to the asphalt he could feel the stored desert heat through his thick Levi jeans.

Most of the drive through this desolate corner of Orange County, California, had been devoid of man-made light, but as Chuck came out of the turn and righted himself, the flat grade of the high desert summit glowed beneath the glare of a truly remarkable canopy of stars. Here, away from any signs of human habitation, away from the strip malls, clogged freeways, and neon-lit gas stations that pockmarked this part of So Cal, the sky was the main attraction. Even through the visor of Chuck's motorcycle helmet, he had to blink to adjust his vision against clusters of stars so bright they seemed splashed across the heavens like fluorescent paint from a twirling brush.

Beneath his bike's wheels, the pavement ended and an area of packed-down sand began. Even so, Chuck was already committed, leaning back in his seat as his hand tightened against the throttle. He gripped the bike with his legs and gunned the engine, shifting himself into a full circus wheelie. His visor flicked up as he skidded forward on that single rear wheel—and over the guttural sound of the bike's gears, he could hear the collective gasp of a group of people in front of him. Twenty-five amateur astronomers were gathered about twenty feet ahead, in a small circle around a half dozen portable telescopes, all sophisticated and expensive. They had at least three Galileo 4.5-inchers, a Meade LT 8-inch, a pair of what looked to be Celestrons—hell, it was hard to tell for sure, up on one wheel. The bike came back down and Chuck hit the brake, coming to a sudden stop. Some of the expressions he read were aghast, others annoyed, but at least a handful of his audience was smiling.

Chuck grinned back at them; he'd been a fairly regular visitor for nearly a decade to these monthly Star Parties thrown by the Orange County Astronomers Organization. Although the faces changed from year to year, he'd developed enough of a reputation to excuse just about any dramatic entrance he could come up with. *Love him, like him, hate him, you certainly couldn't ignore him.* Still grinning, he unhooked his red, white, and blue helmet and shook the sand from his hair. Then he was off the bike, trading the helmet for his own telescope, which was strapped behind his seat above the Honda's rear wheel carriage— a compact Schmidt-Cassegrain with a complementary field tripod—and headed toward the group.

There was a chill in the air at that altitude—forty-three hundred feet—even deep into August, but Chuck was too excited to notice as he greeted the stargazers he recognized and introduced himself to the newcomers. In his thirties, Chuck was a bit older than the average member of the club, which was mostly made up of college and grad school kids, filled out by a handful of hobbyists who'd made the drive down from LA or up from San Diego, but he'd never had any trouble conversing with anyone, of any age. *A talker*, was the way his wife of twelve years, Tammy, always described him, and sometimes she meant it as a compliment.

Ironic, she'd also say, that he'd gone to school for electrical engineering, specifically for designing computer chips, which was so solitary, when all he seemed to want to do when he was out of the house was talk to people. Chuck usually countered that computer chips were pretty good listeners, and they hardly ever walked away.

Everyone continued talking as Chuck went to work on his tripod and gave a percentage of his attention to the precise work of calibrating his telescope. Then again, on a night as clear as this, in a location as prime as Anza, he could have used a paper towel roll and still been able to pick out every constellation in the sky.

The twenty-acre observation site at Anza was one of the main reasons OCAO had grown into the country's largest astronomy club. Chuck had discovered the group—and the relative benefits of the Star Party—after a particularly hairy solo stargazing experience. Before finding Anza, he'd often go by himself to Bell Mountain, near Victorville, California; he'd found a fairly dark area, a clearing in the woods that offered good viewing. On that particular evening, he'd just finished setting up his telescope when he'd heard something moving in the brush behind him. He'd turned around just in time to see a pack of six coyotes stalking toward him. Before he had been able to act, the animals had surrounded him— teeth bared, growling. He'd never been so scared in his life. All he'd had with him to defend himself had been the telescope and a heavy-duty D-cell metal flashlight. He'd seen enough cop shows on TV to know that a flashlight made a pretty good weapon in a pinch, so he'd started waving it, flashing the light in the coyotes' eyes. Then he'd run right toward them, yelling and screaming. To his surprise, the animals had scattered, so he had kept running all the way back to his bike.

Tammy had hoped the coyotes would put an end to Chuck's late-night excursions. She was always worried about his safety up in the mountains. But even a pack of coyotes wasn't going to keep Chuck from his fascination with the sky. Instead, he'd started carrying a single-shot

.22-caliber shotgun with him, strapped beneath the seat of his bike. And he'd found the Anza Star Parties.

Once his telescope was ready, Chuck stepped back, letting one of the other sky gazers—a grad student who worked at the nearby Palomar Observatory—take the first look at a cluster near the base of the Big Dipper. One of the other benefits of the Star Parties, aside from keeping Chuck from getting torn apart by coyotes, was the chance to try out different telescopes; the half dozen scopes spread out among the group represented some of the best portable equipment that overextended credit cards could buy.

But truthfully, Chuck wasn't there that night to test telescopes or, if he was being honest, to look at the stars. He'd seen plenty of stars over a decade of nights like this, and though the telescope and his seeming shared interest in astronomy gave him easy entrance to the stargazing club, his real reason for making the drive up to Anza had only a tangential relationship to the lights in the sky.

"So tell me," he said to the grad student peering through his scope. "You ever see a UFO?"

The grad student laughed.

"A UFO? You mean, like, a flying saucer? Little green men?"

"From what I've heard, they come in all shapes and sizes."

The kid looked up from the telescope. Chuck was smiling amiably, but there was something just a little bit serious behind that smile. The grad student laughed again, then shrugged.

"Hell, everyone's got a story, right? Look at the sky long enough— you're bound to see something that doesn't make a lot of sense."

With that, the kid moved back into the group, toward one of the larger Celestron scopes. Chuck kept on smiling, kept on talking, working through the college students and hobbyists, always finding his way to that same question.

*You ever see a UFO?*

Most of the time, he got laughter, even some eye rolls. The group members who knew him from years past would shake their heads. Chuck being Chuck, they'd think to themselves. And sure, more than a handful believed he was crazy, the young guy with the bike and that red, white, and blue helmet, always asking about UFOs.

But without fail, at least once every Star Party, someone would tell him a story. Maybe right there, in front of the others, or maybe when they were alone. About that one wild night seeing something that was hard to explain. About triangular lights that seemed to come out of no-where, moving at speeds that seemed impossible. About cigar shapes that blinked on and off, a thousand feet up, then disappeared just as suddenly as they had appeared. About spinning, bright flashes that seemed to fly in formation, too damn small to be jets, too damn fast to be helicopters.

And Chuck would nod and listen, and when he walked away, he'd pull his little notepad out of his jacket pocket and write down what he'd heard. When he got home, he'd add the notes to the file cabinet in his cluttered home office, the one room in the house where Tammy didn't go—not because she wasn't allowed, but because she was just a little bit terrified of what she might find in there.

Tammy liked to call Chuck a believer. Inside, he bristled at the des-ignation. He'd always considered himself a reformed skeptic. As long as he could remember, he'd been fascinated by UFOs: unexplained lights in the sky that so many thousands of people had claimed to have seen, all over the world. He wasn't sure where this obsession had started for him or why, even as a child, he'd stayed up late in his backyard staring at the stars, waiting to see something, anything. But by his late teenage years, he'd begun collecting newspaper articles, reading books, and combing through magazines. By his early twenties he'd begun attending the sort of conventions that sprang up around Southern California during the seventies and eighties. At first, they were focused on comic books, then science fiction, and eventually UFOs themselves.

Chuck had become something of an expert on the phenomenon. He knew where the term *UFO* came from: It was first used during the U.S. military's secret investigation into the unexplained sightings—Project Blue Book—that began in 1952 and all the way to 1969, gathering more than 12,600 reports along the way. The description "flying saucer" had an even earlier genesis: June 24, 1947, when a mountain rescue pilot named Kenneth Arnold had chased nine saucerlike objects around Mount Rainier, eventually giving up when the UFOs reached speeds of over twelve hundred miles per hour. He also knew that, officially, the government's interest in UFOs had been halted after the 1968 publication of a two-year-long, military-sponsored study by the University of Colorado called the Condon Report, which had concluded that: "There was no evidence indicating that sightings categorized as 'unidentified' were extraterrestrial vehicles."

The government became reluctant to continue looking into the UFO phenomena, at least openly, and it waited decades before acknowledging it had two other massive investigations—at least—into the subject, Project Sign and Project Grudge. But official disregard did not deter public interest in the subject. Thousands of sightings in the fifties, sixties, and seventies had created a near hysteria in certain circles about the idea of alien visitations. And numerous polls had shown that more than half the population accepted the idea that UFOs were real and of alien origin.

Of course, this did not make it any more acceptable to walk into a room full of strangers and start asking about flying saucers. Tammy wished that Chuck could have kept his obsession a little more private, but Chuck's inquisitiveness was hardwired. His interest—and, indeed, his skepticism—had driven him to become an armchair expert on astronomy, physics, and aerodynamics, whatever might help explain the stories people were telling him. He moved from the science fiction conventions and comic book gatherings to joining the largest national UFO organization—MUFON, the Mutual UFO Network—a UFO-oriented group of more than three thousand paying members and seventy-five "field agents" who were actively investigating sighting reports.

At first, Chuck had been excited to be part of the organization. It was founded by scientists, such as Allen Utke, an associate professor of chemistry at Wisconsin State, and John Schuessler, who had led engineering and space operations at McDonnell Douglas and Boeing. MUFON seemed to be a nonprofit that had taken over where Project Blue Book had left off, and Chuck had eagerly attended numerous MUFON conventions. He had taken the required test on UFO lore to gain premier membership, and he paid his dues in exchange for the monthly MUFON magazine, which included details about numerous UFO sightings around the country.

But Chuck became disenchanted by the politics within the organization itself. Maybe because it was always in search of financing from outside sources, MUFON seemed to him to have a shifting agenda beyond the publicizing of evidence of outer-worldly phenomena. The field agents seemed adept at gathering information, but where that information went seemed murky. MUFON didn't have its own laboratories to study any evidence its agents brought in, and few actual scientists were available to examine anything substantial; first responders to UFO sightings who collected what appeared to be charred topsoil or unidentifiable fragments had to find outside labs with facilities for chemical analysis. On top of that, there were rumors that MUFON had CIA or other government ties at the highest levels, including a director who reportedly had been in the CIA and had connections to the organization's Moscow bureau. Though Chuck wasn't usually a conspiracy theorist, he had enough questions of his own about the organization to want to keep his distance. He'd put his membership on hold and hadn't moved forward in trying to become one of their official field agents.

Chuck decided to follow a more grassroots, individualist approach. Every morning and afternoon—even sometimes during his lunch hour at work at a midlevel microchip firm—he'd scour newspapers, check Internet boards, searching for anything that mentioned UFOs or unexplained sightings. Then he'd do the same in person, at Star Parties like Anza, at the conventions in LA and San Diego, even at the monthly MUFON gatherings. And if he was lucky enough to hear or read about a UFO site within three hundred miles of his home, he'd tell Tammy to start packing the family suitcases.

*Bright lights, flying saucers, and little green men.* Glancing down into the lens of his portable telescope, eyes adjusting to the brilliant splashes of light painted across the ink-black sky, Chuck knew, deep down, he was chasing something bigger than his own internal need to believe.

And, hell, hobby or obsession or whatever Tammy wanted to call it, Chuck figured there were plenty of worse ways to spend his free time.

# CHAPTER 4

RHINE VALLEY,
GERMAN-OCCUPIED TERRITORY,
NOVEMBER 1944

At 250 mph, nothing was textbook—especially in the dead of night, a thousand feet above the twisting black water of the Rhine, banking in and out of thick clouds, turbulent air rushing against the cockpit as the instruments across multiple dashes clicked and hummed in a symphony of controlled electricity.

Beneath the bubble of crack-proof glass, U.S. Army Air Force Lieutenant Ed Schleuter hunched over the controls of his Northrop P-61 Black Widow, his eyes peeled to take in the complicated terrain below, searching for ghostlike wisps of smoke that might indicate a German supply train or a factory exhaust stack. At the moment, he felt so damn *alive*, maybe because every minute seemed borrowed; he knew the statistics, how dangerous—damn crazy, in fact—these night missions were. One in three pilots who took to the air didn't make it back to base; that was a simple fact, but Lieutenant Schleuter wasn't the sort of man to let facts, no matter how horrifying, color his sense of duty.

The night flights weren't just heroic, they were necessary. Pioneered by the British in their elegant Bristol Beaufighters, these missions had become increasingly important to the Allied war effort. The Germans knew that by day, the Americans and Brits increasingly ruled the skies, making the movement of troops and materials almost impossible. For more than a year now, the Beaufighters had taken the cover of night away from the Germans as well—and now that the Yanks had arrived, there was no way they were going to let the British continue to have all the fun.

Schleuter might have been crazy, but that didn't mean he was careless. In addition to watching for the supply trains and factories, he was also keeping a lookout for the tangled forests and rising hills that jutted upward on either side of the snaking river. Compared to the Beaufighters, his P-61 was a beast, bristling with cannons and machine guns; but it would crumple and burn just as fast if he hit something at these speeds. His radar operator, Don Meiers, seated in a sunken well behind his pilot's perch, was one of the best, but Schleuter knew from experience that flying by radar was still far from a perfect science.

"Lieutenant, are you seeing what I'm seeing? What the hell are those lights?"

Schleuter jerked up from the controls as the unfamiliar voice burst over his comm system; then he remembered the third man who had taken to the air with them that evening, a last-minute addition who had put himself on the roster, much to Schleuter's dismay. Lieutenant Fred Ringwald, now seated in the gunner pod, was Air Force intelligence. Which meant he pretty much did whatever he wanted, without explanation, including tagging along on a night mission. Schleuter didn't like having someone he barely knew on board, but so far, the intelligence officer had been a silent observer, allowing Schleuter and his radar operator the space they needed to keep the team as safe as possible as they searched out targets on either side of the Rhine. Now, obviously, that was going to change.

Schleuter shifted his attention back to the controls.

"I'm sure they're stars," he said. "Break in the clouds, you see a lot of stars."

"Those aren't stars. There must be ten of them. And they're moving right toward us."

The hair on the back of Schleuter's neck suddenly stood up, and he quickly looked up from the controls.

"Where?"

"Starboard, closing fast."

Schleuter shifted his eyes to the left, alert but still moderately skeptical. If there was something out there at altitude, he would have heard it from Meiers first, or from the ground, where multiple radar bases were tracking their progress.

"I don't see . . ."

He stopped midsentence.

*Christ.* The intelligence officer was right, there were ten of them, spaced in what had to be a controlled formation. *Bright orange balls of light.* Almost fiery, nearly perfectly circular. And they were moving directly toward the P-61.

"Could that be a reflection?" Ringwald asked.

It was easy to be fooled by tricks of light, reflections off clouds or unexpected high-altitude bodies of water, even reflections off other planes. But there were differences.

Schleuter said, "I don't think so. Not the way they're moving. Meiers . . ."

"Lieutenant," the radar operator hissed, the tension thick in his voice. "There's nothing up here. I mean, I see them, but I promise you, there's nothing on the radar. Not a goddamn blip."

Schleuter grabbed the rudder in front of him and began banking them hard, directly toward the lights. He didn't know what they were, but he wasn't going to run: He was going to put the guns on them as fast as he could. Even as he turned the plane toward the orange lights, he hit the comm that connected him to the closest ground radar. He quickly gave his codes, then asked if they had anything on their scopes.

"No bogies," was the instant response. "You're alone up there."

Schleuter whistled low, now facing the ten orange fireballs, which were getting larger by the second.

"Please repeat," he said into the comm. "You don't see anything in our vicinity?"

"No bogies. Lieutenant, are you okay?"

Schleuter flicked the comm off and pushed the yoke forward, moving toward their top speed of 360 mph. The wind was roaring against the cockpit now, the fiery orange lights growing bigger and bigger and bigger.

And then, suddenly, they vanished. Schleuter gasped out loud, but kept both hands on the controls, sending the P-61 barreling toward where he'd last seen the lights. The plane cut through the distance in seconds, and then they were right where the fireballs should have been. *Nothing.* Whatever they were, they had simply blinked out of existence.

*Impossible.* Schleuter had been flying for most of his adult life. He had trained on dozens of different types of planes and had an expert's knowledge of the technology that existed. And what he'd just seen—it was impossible.

He began to turn the plane back on course, and was reaching for the comm to reconnect with the ground when the intelligence officer's voice hit him again from the gunner dome.

"What the hell? Lieutenant—starboard, again."

Schleuter turned to the left and saw that the lights were back. But this time they were at three times the distance. He could still make them out, ten fiery balls of orange, moving in formation, but far away. Impossibly far away.

Nothing could move that far, that fast, under control.

"Incredible," the intelligence officer whispered. But now there was something odd in Ringwald's voice. He sounded impressed, but not entirely *surprised*.

"Is there something you want to tell me?" Schleuter said.

The intelligence officer didn't respond.

This wasn't the first time these lights had been seen during a night flight; in fact, these sightings had been going on since the beginning of the war. Eventually, an officer in Schleuter's own unit, the 415th Night Fighter Squadron, would give this bizarre phenomenon a name. The officer, an avid fan of a comic strip called *Smokey Stover*, would borrow from one of the comic's signature lines: "Where's there's foo, there's fire," and from then on, the strange lights would become known as "Foo Fighters." By the end of the war, the Foo Fighters were so prevalent, newspapers around the world, including the *New York Times*, heralded their existence.

Alone in the cockpit of the P-61, rattled but still on mission, Schleuter didn't know any of this; he had seen something that didn't make any sense. His mind whirled through possibilities—was it some bizarre technology the Germans had thought up, some strange, controllable missile or aeronautic vessel, maybe some new twist of psychological warfare? Whatever those fiery balls were, they hadn't damaged his plane, but they had certainly tangled his nerves.

Even so, he decided that he wasn't going to be filing any report when he got back to base, and he'd advise Meiers to follow his lead. The intelligence officer could take whatever they'd seen to whomever he wanted— but Schleuter sure as hell wasn't going to risk his career by telling crazy stories about fireballs in the sky.

At 250 mph, nothing was textbook.

Not even close.*

---

* *The Hunt for Zero Point: Inside the Classified World of Antigravity Technology,* by Nick Cook (U.S.A.: Broadway Books, 2003), pp. 39–41.

## BALLS OF FIRE STALK U.S. FIGHTERS IN NIGHT ASSAULTS OVER GERMANY

*— New York Times,* 1-2-45

The Germans have thrown something new into the night skies over Germany—the weird, mysterious "foo-fighter," balls of fire that race alongside the wings of American fighters flying intruder missions over the Reich. American pilots have been encountering the eerie "foo-fighter" for more than a month in their night flights. No one apparently knows exactly what this sky weapon is.

The balls of fire appear suddenly and accompany the planes for miles. They appear to be radio-controlled from the ground and keep up with planes flying 300 miles an hour, official intelligence reports reveal. "There are three kinds of these lights we call 'foo-fighters,'" Lieut. Donald Meiers of Chicago said. "One is red balls of fire which appear off our wing tips and fly along with us; the second is a vertical row of three balls of fire which fly in front of us, and the third is a group of about fifteen lights which appear off in the distance—like a Christmas tree up in the air—and flicker on and off."

The pilots of this night-fighter squadron—in operation since September, 1943—find these fiery balls the weirdest thing that they have yet encountered. They are convinced that the "foo-fighter" is designed to be a psychological as well as a military weapon, although it is not the nature of the fire-balls to attack planes.

"A 'foo-fighter' picked me up recently at 700 feet and chased me twenty miles down the Rhine Valley," Lt. Meiers said. "I turned to starboard and two balls of fire turned with me. I turned to the port side and they turned with me. We were going 260 miles an hour and the balls were keeping right up with us.

"On another occasion when a 'foo-fighter' picked us up, I dove at 360 miles per hour. It kept right off our wing tips for awhile and then zoomed up into the sky.

"When I first saw the things off my wing tips, I had the horrible thought that a German on the ground was ready to press a button and explode them. But they don't explode or attack us. They just seem to follow us like will-o'-the-wisps."

Lt. Wallace Gould of Silver Creek, NY said that the lights had followed his wing tips for a while and then, in a few seconds, zoomed 20,000 feet into the air out of sight. Lt. Edward Schlater of Oshkosh, Wisconsin, said that he had seen the "foo-fighter" on two occasions and it "looked like shooting stars." In his first experience with them, Lt. Gould said, "I thought it was some new form of jet-propulsion plane after us. But we were very close to them and none of us saw any structure on the fire balls."

After several of these reports—and after the end of the war—few pilots came forward to admit to further sightings of Foo Fighters.

But others did.

# CHAPTER 5

## ROSWELL, NEW MEXICO,
## JUNE 1994

Through the darkness, Chuck Zukowski could see the smoke—wisps and trickles at first, rising from within the fracture lines in the densely packed sand. The smoke seemed odd, almost alive, pushed out from beneath the desert floor according to some internal rhythm. Then, as the darkness was suddenly broken by flickering lights—green and yellow streaks flashing across the whitened sand—the smoke thickened into plumes and tendrils, billowing fingers reaching right out toward where Chuck was standing. But he didn't move. He stood transfixed by the scene that was suddenly illuminated in front of him: the huge silver disk hanging frozen above the dune, the four strange gray aliens coming out of the smoke, each approximately four feet tall, with bulbous heads, cat eyes, spindly arms and legs.

"Well, this is a bit much, isn't it?"

Chuck's gaze was broken as Tammy pointed past him toward the closest alien in the diorama.

"I mean that guy looks almost happy. His spaceship is about to crash-land, and at least one of his crew is lying dead in that glass case over there in front of Daniel, about to get autopsied. You'd think he'd be pretty pissed off."

Despite himself, Chuck had to grin. He inhaled, tasting the cheap special-effect smoke on the back of his tongue. Maybe Tammy was right, maybe the diorama in front of him—the ten-foot-square sandy desert scene, the flying saucer and smiling gray aliens—was a bit kitschy, but to Chuck, it was Christmas in June. He had been dreaming about standing right there, behind that waist-high red velvet rope, in this place that seemed so much like the center of his own personal universe, for as long as he could remember.

Chuck looked from the alien in front of him to the transparent coffin, holding a shriveled plastic and rubber body in a simulated autopsy scene of an alien on the other side of the rectangular display room. His eight-year-old son, Daniel, was surreptitiously trying to pry his way beneath the glass, and beyond that, his oldest son, Chuck Jr., was looking as bored as only an overly mature twelve-year-old could standing in front of a wall full of black-and-white photos depicting World War II Foo Fighters. But Chuck's five-year-old daughter, Ashley, was all smiles as she poked at a 1950s-era anthropomorphic air force crash test dummy that was hanging from a metal hook, beneath a panel describing the various conspiracy theories involving government agencies determined to keep UFOs in the realm of pulp science fiction.

He turned back to his wife, shrugging.

"I'm sure this particular alien has an advanced enough sense of humor to see the irony in his situation. Zooming along in a highly sophisticated spaceship, traveling millions of light-years across deep, lonely space, only to get blasted out of the sky by a thunderstorm, crash-land on some backwoods ranch, his wreck carted off by horseback and then in flatbed trucks, the debris eventually mistaken for a weather balloon. If you can't smile at that, you may as well just volunteer for the autopsy and get it over with."

Tammy rolled her eyes as she moved to corral the kids before they did any real damage to the exhibits or disturbed the half dozen other midday patrons of the museum, who seemed mostly glazed and dazed by the sights around them. Chuck couldn't blame them; when he'd entered the museum from Main Street, he'd spent his first few minutes frozen just inside, eyes as wide as the fake crashed saucer.

Part of him couldn't believe he was even there. The entire three-day trip from Southern California had been part dream, part experiment; he still wasn't sure how he had convinced Tammy to trade in the 1990 family Ford Aerostar van for the twenty-four-foot Winnebago that was now parked sideways in a corner of the museum's parking lot, taking up at least three spots, two wheels touching the curb. Officially, they'd bought the massive RV so they could vacation relatively cheaply together as a family; but Chuck's real motivation was to incorporate his UFO research and investigations into those family vacations. This trip, culminating here, at the International UFO Museum in Roswell, New Mexico—the beating heart of the UFO world—was the Zukowski clan's maiden journey. The three-day expedition began at Meteor Crater, Arizona, off Interstate 40, so the kids could see what a meteor the size of a Volkswagen could do when it hit the ground. Then on to the underground Ice Caves in Grants, New Mexico, a natural "icebox" rock formation where the temperature remained the same throughout the year, and where various American Indian artifacts had been discovered dating back over a thousand years that seem to show supernatural beings. On to the White Sands National Monument, where the kids could now play in the white sand, near the once-secret and infamous missile base—site of the 1945 Trinity explosion—that shares the monument's name.

Chuck had been thrilled to see how well the kids and Tammy had taken to life on the road; sleeping, eating, even showering in the RV or at the odd, low-cost motel. He was touched that they indulged him as he waxed eloquent about the various paranormal and extraterrestrial hot spots that they drove by. But still, nothing along the way could have prepared him for the feelings that had overwhelmed him when they'd finally reached Roswell.

Chuck Zukowski

Navigating the RV down Main Street, trying to avoid the parked cars on either side on his way to the International UFO Museum, Chuck had had the strange feeling that he was about to open a door he'd been knocking at his entire life.

Even the kids had sensed that this stop on their road trip was going to be something different. As the two-story museum surged into view on the other side of the panoramic windshield of the Winnebago, Daniel poked his head into the front from the interior of the vehicle, shouting over the sound of his older brother's boom box: "Is this gonna be one of Dad's talking trips?"

Chuck had been about to cut off Tammy's imminent answer with one of his own when Ashley pushed Daniel aside, holding up a stuffed gray alien she'd picked up in the gift aisle of a gas station they'd visited just outside the Roswell town limits.

"Don't listen to him, Daddy. You go right ahead and talk to everybody. Mr. Chalupa likes your stories."

Chuck had grinned at his daughter and the plush alien, framed in the planklike rearview mirror of the RV. Some kids collected stuffed bunny rabbits or puppies; his five-year-old daughter carried an alien that she'd named after a kind of taco. But he didn't have much time to ruminate on the amount of therapy he was likely setting his kids up for, because the next thing he knew he was parking the RV and leading his family through the doors of the museum. He felt like a kid in his own personal toy store. He'd paid the small fee to the elderly woman behind the front desk and then was swept up in all the UFO paraphernalia—the saucer and alien dioramas; the various poster boards covered in newspaper clippings of UFO sightings; a roped-off area containing replicas of the radar technology that had first sighted the original craft that had supposedly gone down just outside the town's limits; even Mayan and American Indian artifacts that seemed to document an ancient connection to extraterrestrial fires and lights in the skies.

It wasn't until he and Tammy reached the largest of the dioramas—the saucer and its Mr. Chalupa–like occupants—that he'd finally started to segue from awed tourist to amateur tour guide. Of course, the minute he'd begun really talking his way through the displays, the boys, and even Ashley, had scattered like debris from a crashed ship. Tammy was at least humoring him. She didn't have to believe in UFOs to understand that something unusual had occurred in Roswell.

"So supposedly that's what happened?" she asked, after pulling Daniel away from the autopsy scene and placing him in front of some models of B-29 bombers—the same sort of plane that had been used to transfer the debris to a different air force base in Dallas. "A flying saucer got caught in a thunderstorm?"

Chuck shrugged again.

"As the story goes, beginning at the end of June 1947, after Kenneth Arnold saw his original 'flying saucers' over Mount Rainier, the military had gone on high alert, using fixed radar to search for anything strange in the skies. Around the night of July 3, radar operators at Walker Base in Roswell—a significant place because it was our country's first nuclear base, where the crew of the *Enola Gay* trained, and where the B-29s that dropped the atomic bombs on Japan were stationed—began tracking a pair of strange objects flying in formation."

"UFOs," Tammy said, pointing to the black-and-white images above Chuck Jr., who had amazingly remained in the same place for what had to be close to two minutes, a new record.

"Like the flying objects—Foo Fighters—World War II pilots used to report seeing. They were unidentifiable, and they were objects, and they were moving fast enough that it took radar from three different bases to try to stay on top of them. But then this massive storm moved in—lightning, thunder, the kind of crazy squall they get around here—and the objects disappeared. And that's when the rancher and the horses come in."

Chuck ushered Tammy toward one of the poster boards, filled with black-and-white photos. One showed a ranch house at the center of a field, another the chiseled visage of a rancher. Chuck let Tammy read the basics of the rest of the story herself—he had gone through it so many times on his own, he knew all the beats by heart. July 3, 1947, forty-eight-year-old rancher Mac Brazel and his eight-year-old son were waiting out a massive lightning storm at the Hines ranch house, eighty miles northwest of Roswell. The next morning, they'd ventured out on horseback to check on their sheep—and had come across an enormous debris site, stretching over three hundred yards across a gouged pasture. Brazel had tucked some of the debris under his hat, then had ridden to a nearby ranch owned by his neighbors and friends, the Proctors. More debris was brought to the Proctors' ranch by horseback and examined. The debris seemed strange—thin, flexible, metallic materials that couldn't be broken or burned, long cross-beams that seemed to have strange, colored, hieroglyphiclike writing on them, nothing that resembled wires or electronics. The rancher and his friends had no idea what they'd found, but they knew it was unusual.

So Mac had ridden over to the nearest town, Corona, and had called Sheriff Wilcox in Roswell. In turn, the sheriff had contacted Roswell Army Air Force Base. And that's where the story took an interesting turn.

"See, the Air Force knew that something real had happened out there," Chuck said, unable to contain himself long enough to let Tammy finish reading. "Because they'd been tracking the UFOs themselves. They immediately ordered a decorated intelligence officer and radar engineer, Jesse Marcel, and a member of the Counter Intelligence Corps, Sheridan Cavitt, out to the debris site. Marcel and Cavitt collected as much of the material as they could, filling a flatbed truck with the stuff, and took it back to base. They also reported seeing the same strange metallic materials, unbreakable and unburnable, the odd hieroglyphic writing. The base commander, Colonel William Blanchard, investigated the materials himself—and then ordered his first lieutenant, officer Walter Haut, to put out a press release."

Tammy had gotten to the release herself, and Chuck was pleased to see the surprised expression on her face as she read the headline.

**"RAAF CAPTURES FLYING SAUCER ON RANCH IN ROSWELL REGION."**

"That just about says it all, doesn't it?"
Tammy read the rest of the release to herself:

> The many rumors regarding the flying discs became a reality yesterday when the intelligence office of the 509th (atomic) Bomb Group of the 8th Air Force, Roswell Army Air Field, was fortunate enough to gain possession of a disc through the cooperation of one of the ranchers and the sheriff's office of Chaves county. The flying object landed on a ranch near Roswell sometime last week.

"This was a military press release? For real?"
Chuck nodded.
"It was carried on the front page of the *Roswell Daily Record*, then by newspapers across the country: the *Los Angeles Herald*, the *San Fran-*

*cisco Chronicle*, the *Sacramento Bee*, the *Seattle Daily Times*, and on and on. You have to remember, this was right after the war, the beginning of the Cold War. Two years after the first nuclear explosion—for the military to announce something like this, to put something like this out in the open, either they were pretty sure they had found something earth-shattering, or they had made one hell of a mistake."

Tammy pointed to a photo on an adjacent poster board—of Jesse Marcel, the radar operator who had first investigated the debris, posing in front of the remains of an experimental weather balloon.

"Seems to me that the air force quickly decided it was the latter," she commented.

On the surface, she was correct. After the Haut press release, Marcel had been ordered to load the debris onto one of the 509th's B-29 Superfortress bombers and transport it to Wright Field in Dayton, Ohio. But during the flight, Marcel was told to make a quick stop at the Eighth Air Force headquarters in Fort Worth, Texas. At the Fort Worth Army Air Field, a new investigation of the debris took place, under General

United States Air Force/AFP/Getty Images

Roger Ramey, the commander of the Eighth Air Force. There, it was offi-cially determined that the debris had come from a crashed experimental weather balloon—part of a top-secret Mogul project to monitor nuclear explosions from other countries—specifically, Russia.

"Officially, the story changed—it wasn't a UFO, it was a weather bal-loon. A balloon that somehow a decorated intelligence officer special-izing in radar targets misidentified. A balloon—made out of strange, unbreakable metal with pieces covered in hieroglyphics."

Chuck didn't bother to add that Marcel himself, in later years, had admitted that the official photo had been staged—that the debris in the picture was not from the crash site at all but had been brought in by Ramey to bolster the fabricated weather balloon story. Nevertheless, by the end of that afternoon, the air force's original press release had been rescinded. A second press release was issued, stating that the 509th Bomb Group had mistakenly identified a weather balloon as wreckage of a flying saucer.

Meanwhile, uniformed crews had hastily cleared the debris. On hands and knees, airmen combed through the crash site, the Hines ranch, anywhere Brazel and any other witnesses might have taken pieces from the crash—crating everything and reportedly moving all of it to a hangar in the nearby air force base. According to UFO legend, from there the debris was moved to the country's most secret military research base, which was located eighty miles northwest of Las Vegas, Nevada—Area 51, a base so covert the government still—in 1994—didn't even acknowl-edge it existed. From that point forward, the military likewise denied any knowledge of a UFO crash in Roswell. But that didn't keep Roswell from becoming a household name—and forever connected to the UFO phenomenon.

Tammy began gathering the kids—she planned on taking them back to the RV for lunch, giving Chuck some alone time at the museum to conduct research, to talk his way around the room. He wondered how much of the story had breached her skepticism, but doubted that much beyond the retracted press release had given her pause. The jump from radar blips and lights in the sky to flying saucers was asking a lot, no matter how many military files Chuck could show her, or how many eyewitness testimonies filled the museum. And the jump from flying saucers to aliens . . . Chuck smiled to himself as he turned back toward the diorama in the center of the room.

To his surprise, directly past the four "Grays" gathered beneath the crashing saucer, he saw a face he recognized from his own research: Glenn Dennis—one of the founders of the museum, the mortician who had worked at the nearby Ballard Funeral Home in Roswell. Dennis had become part of the Roswell story shortly after the rescinded press release, when, reportedly, he had been contacted by the air force, which, mysteriously, had been searching for hermetically sealed, child-sized coffins. According to what Chuck had read, Dennis claimed to have been brought into the air force base hospital, where he had been shown pieces of strange wreckage and had met with a nurse who had told him about bodies that had been found at a second crash site, located a few klicks from where Brazel had found his debris.

Seeing Dennis in person, Chuck felt rooted to the floor. He could still hear Tammy ushering the kids toward the door, but his focus homed in on the elderly mortician. This wasn't just some affidavit or witness testimony on a piece of aging paper, this was a first-person player in one of the central stories of UFO lore. Dennis was living history.

Chuck quickly headed around the diorama and approached Dennis. After introducing himself, Chuck told Dennis how important he felt the Roswell incident was, how many secrets and stories had emanated from that one incident, how in many ways, all roads in UFOlogy lead back to Roswell. It was a short conversation, much of it lost in a rush of nervous energy. Chuck couldn't be sure, but he felt that he had at least made a connection, one that he'd try, in the future, to nurture. He wasn't sure where a friendship with a man like Dennis might lead, but as he thanked the mortician for his time and headed back into the depths of the museum, he had a feeling that he had taken an important first step.

Chuck spent the rest of his day talking to museum staff and visitors and thumbing through eyewitness affidavits, many of which had multiple blacked-out sentences, evidence redacted by unknown military overseers for threatening national security—god only knew how or why. By late afternoon, he was back with his family in the RV, heading down Main Street toward the old Roswell Army Air Field. After first passing right by the Ballard Funeral Home, the place where Dennis had worked when the incident had occurred, they finally reached the airfield, once known as Walker Air Force Base and long since closed to the public. The base's nondescript, unmarked hangars were surrounded by a high, barbed-wire fence. All Chuck could do was drive the RV around the perimeter, staring at each low-slung building, trying to figure out which might once have housed wreckage, which might have concealed a handful of child-sized bodies.

Tammy may not have believed that anything had occurred in this place beyond a lightning storm and a mistaken military press release, but for Chuck, that barbed-wire fence told him everything he needed to know about UFOs, the military, and Roswell.

Some things made it into press releases, however briefly. And some things remained secret, obscured—and unexplained—for a very long time.

# CHAPTER 6

"There isn't any blood," Glenda said, her voice trembling.

Chuck dropped to one knee by the closest, partially stripped corpse, the larger of the two dead horses—the male named Buck. His rubber gloves felt snug around his fingers as he sealed them tight at his wrists.

She was correct—the animals had been drained of blood. No reddened stains anywhere on the revealed bones, the mostly intact rib cage, skull, and stripped limbs. There did appear to be a darkened area of ground just in front of the dead horse, and below its hooves—and in the police report Chuck had read, the investigating officers had called it a pool of blood—but Glenda and Chuck were both experienced enough with dead animals to know the difference between decomposing fats and other bodily fluids and blood. A horse like this—a large male, maybe twelve hundred pounds before whatever happened to it—should have contained about four gallons of blood. For whatever reason, this horse had been exsanguinated—either before it was killed, or after.

"Not enough blood on the ground," Chuck noted, "and none on the body."

Now with both knees in the dirt in front of the animal, Chuck leaned forward, his gloved fingers gingerly reaching toward Buck's partially skinned torso.

38

Chuck Zukowski

"Looks like a long, T-like incision going down what's left of the abdominal area," he said, talking mostly to himself, focusing on the areas of the carcass where he could still see flesh and memorizing what he would eventually put in his field notebook, which he'd then share with his expert veterinary contacts at the University of Colorado. "The back anal area was cut out in an unusual circular manner, void of the penis. The eyes, the tongue—and again, not the expected blood pooling, even with such a massive wound."

Strange, perhaps impossibly so—even days later, there should have been blood around these wounds.

When Chuck had first talked to Glenda on the phone before he'd driven over to Rush, the woman had called the incisions on her horses "laserlike," and had described a burn-type smell associated with them. And in the police report, the officers had related being led onto the scene by Glenda's husband, who had been agitatedly suggesting that some sort of military agency must have been responsible for the butchery, using high-tech lasers. Chuck took a deep breath, then shook his head.

"I don't see any burn markings," he said, running his gloved fingers along each revealed rib. "No signs of cauterization at all."

And there was no scent of burning flesh or bone; whatever smell had once been associated with the wounds had since cleared. However, as Chuck continued running his fingers along each of the animal's ribs, he felt grooves. He peered closely and noticed unusual, etchlike markings, starting approximately three inches from the spine on each rib, origi- nating up near the skull, and running consistently down all the ribs, a straight-line pattern leading all the way to the eleventh rib.

*Curious.* He kept the grooves to himself, as he rose from his knees and shifted to the second horse, splayed out in an identical position. He was pretty sure that when he eventually got out his measuring tape, he'd find the positioning so precise, the differences would be minuscule.

He didn't even need to go to his knees to see that Princess's wounds were also nearly identical to Buck's; the same partially excavated hide, the same missing eyes, tongue, and anal region, the same bizarre lack of blood. After making mental notes, Chuck reached back into his equip- ment pack and retrieved his EMF reader. Glenda took a step closer as he handled the sophisticated-looking gear.

"I know," he said, fiddling with the settings as he extended the micro- phonelike receiver. "Looks like something out of *Star Trek*. It's a Trifield EMF reader. Picks up residual energy on surfaces and in the air. Electri- cians use them to find wiring in walls, electric hot spots in old buildings. Sometimes the FBI even uses them to look for bugs—listening devices— in cars and homes. I've set this one to filter out a base level of natural and man-made electromagnetic fields, so I can look for anything unusual."

The rancher nodded, but Chuck was fairly certain his explanation was mostly noise to her. As an engineer by training, Chuck was proud of this particular piece of equipment; it had cost more than four hundred dollars, and he'd purchased it retail from the same manufacturer who made the circuit readers he used at his day job at a midlevel microchip firm in Colorado Springs. Tammy had nearly kicked him out of the house when she'd found the bill for the EMF reader in his wallet. He'd had to take her to Home Depot for a new set of countertops for the kitchen to get back in her good graces, though he was still trying to figure out how he was going to pay for them. But the EMF reader was a necessity; the Trifield could pick up any residual energy from sources electronic, magnetic, or radio. If something truly unnatural had occurred on this ranch, the EMF reader could provide what he considered real, tangible evidence.

Once the device was set at the correct levels, Chuck carefully ran the receiver over Princess, starting at the animal's hooves and then moving up to the bottom of the rib cage, close near the spine where he'd found the odd grooves. Almost immediately, the electromagnetic levels jumped, starting around eight microteslas at the bottom ribs, rising past ten microteslas as Chuck got closer to the skull. Chuck could feel Glenda leaning over his shoulder, watching the measurement arrows dancing across the EMF reader's display screen.

"That normal?"

"Actually, no. In my opinion, these are noticeable levels. Something involving electronics took place here."

Especially considering this was nearly a week after the event, Chuck could only guess how high these readings might have been within the first twenty-four hours. He cursed inwardly; it was truly frustrating, the idea that there was so much lag time between when one of these incidents happened and when he learned about it. Scouring newspapers, reading MUFON circulars, even getting direct calls from the sources he'd cultivated—it wasn't enough. He needed to find a way to increase his access to events closer to when they occurred.

Still, for the moment, he had to work with what was in front of him. And if the EMF readings were as significant as he believed, what was in front of him was pretty damn incredible.

"This is goddamn bizarre, isn't it?" Glenda asked.

The fear was back in her voice. Chuck turned off the EMF reader and rose to his feet. As he removed his gloves, he tried to put on his calmest, most reassuring expression. He understood this woman's fear. Third-generation ranchers sure as hell knew how animals were supposed to die. And when they saw an animal—a horse, a part of the family—dead in a way they didn't comprehend, it was terrifying.

Worse yet, as bizarre as the two corpses were, this was not a unique crime scene. In fact, though Chuck wasn't going to bring it up with Glenda, this particular mutilation scene was especially significant because of its location.

The very first well-publicized mutilation had occurred very close to Glenda's ranch, more than fifty years earlier. Back in 1967, a horse named Lady had been killed and similarly excised in nearby Alamosa, Colorado. Lady's head and neck had been skinned, and her hide appeared to have been cauterized. As with Buck and Princess, the wounds had been bloodless.

That particular mutilation had also been accompanied by a handful of UFO sightings, within a twenty-four-hour period. One witness, a superior court judge named Charles Bennett, had claimed to have seen "three reddish orange rings in the sky" that had maintained a triangular formation and had moved at incredible speeds. These reports had galvanized popular interest.

That 1967 incident, so close to where Glenda had found her prized horses, had caused the phenomenon of animal mutilations to enter the paranormal lexicon.

Standing next to the two dead horses—the terrified whine of the rancher's dog still rising above the wind—Chuck did his best to reassure Glenda that he was going to do everything he could to try to help her understand what had happened on her ranch. He would run as many tests as he could on the two corpses, perhaps even cart the carcasses over to his veterinary sources at the university, and take readings on the "surviving" horse, as well as the traumatized dog. But even so, he was certain that nothing he could say or do would be enough. In fact, at the moment, nothing anyone could say, or do, would be enough.

In Chuck's expert opinion—and over the past eight years, he had turned himself into one of the most knowledgeable investigators in the world—the scene in front of them wasn't the result of a predator. No animal could have caused these bizarre wounds. Nor did Chuck see any evidence that pointed to human culpability. No footprints, tire tracks, or signs of violence one would expect with two horses taken down like this, in such close proximity, in such a macabre manner.

In their report, the two officers who had first investigated the scene agreed it wasn't a predator, and despite any actual evidence, had assumed it was some sort of act of animal cruelty. Chuck believed their report only opened doors to more questions than it answered: In the history of animal mutilations—ten thousand, over the past fifty years—nobody had ever been caught or arrested.

*Every one of them had eventually been deemed unexplained.*

"But you've seen this before," Glenda said. "How could this be happening, over and over again, and nobody knows why?"

Why? How? This was a phenomenon so vast there were cases being recorded in more than a half dozen states, sometimes simultaneously, sometimes as many as ten in a week.

"What about the authorities? Not the local cops, I mean, like maybe the sheriff, the mayor's office?"

Chuck pulled off his rubber gloves and put his hand on Glenda's trembling shoulder, leading her back to the house.

"Actually, it's gone a lot higher than that."

In fact, the phenomenon of animal mutilations, which had been simultaneously mocked as the product of some sort of midwestern mass hysteria and shrouded in continually redacted secrecy, had once inspired a massive, multistate investigation. It had involved a Democratic senator from Colorado, the FBI, at least one satanic cult, and a near decade-long open case file that had ended right back where it had started.

*Ten thousand animal mutilations—all of them unexplained.*

# CHAPTER 7

## SEDONA, ARIZONA, AND TAOS, NEW MEXICO, JULY 1996

36.3940° N, 105.5767° W

Chuck took the corner a little faster than he had to, the jeep's tires screeching as they gripped the road. Tammy had both hands flat against the dashboard between them, pinning the travel brochure wide open with her palms as the desert wind whipped through the four-wheel-drive vehicle's wide-open chassis, fighting to pull the glossy material right out the window.

"It's just as spiritual at twenty miles per hour as it is at sixty-five," Tammy shouted over the sound of the jeep's engine. "If you keep this up and I lose the map, we're going to end up in Nevada. Or at the very least, spending the evening in some Indian reservation. Are you sure we haven't passed it yet?"

Chuck shook his head, his hair ruffling in the wind. Although the sun had gone down hours ago, he knew by the stars above what direction he was going—and in truth, he didn't really care if he took a few wrong turns. Sedona was one of those places where the journey really was the

44

destination. One of the most beautiful spots on Earth, its landscape was beyond anything Chuck had ever seen on their other family road trips.

Off to the left, a pair of giant rock outcroppings rose right out of the sand to parallel heights of maybe thirty feet, like the legs of some ancient stone colossus, sheared off at the knees. To his right, a low field of chiseled boulders, a reddish moonscape ending at the feet of another rock monolith, arching backward beneath the lunar glare.

Glancing in the rearview mirror, Chuck only wished the kids had stayed awake a little longer. The stunning geography of this desert, strewn with so many magnificent, unique red sandstone towers and cliffs, formed by millions of years of wind, sun, and sand—the Earth itself literally evolving in front of your eyes—was even more impressive at night. The giant shapes flashing along the highway seemed almost alive.

On the other hand, Chuck couldn't blame the three of them, now fast asleep in a spaghetti jumble of little limbs and hair in the backseat of the jeep, for missing one moment among many. Sedona wasn't the first stop on this particular excursion, which had actually begun in New Mexico, a little ways down Interstate 40 from Albuquerque.

At the beginning of the trip, it hadn't just been Chuck's immediate family. Tammy's parents, Jim and Linda Inman, had been along for the ride. Although it had all started innocently enough, a short vacation by way of the RV to see the Indian pueblos and play a little golf in the desert, somehow Chuck had convinced the family to make a diversion to the town of Taos, a small artists' community just south of Wheeler Peak, along a tributary of the Rio Grande. Aside from its art galleries, fishing, and mountain hikes, Taos also happened to be known in the UFO community because of a strange phenomenon—*the Hum*—that Chuck had been reading about for many years.

The Hum was a persistent, low-frequency rumble that only certain people could hear, indoors and out. It began and ended suddenly, and it wasn't unique to Taos. Similar Hum hot spots had been reported in various locations around the globe, including Kokomo, Indiana, West Seattle, even Auckland, New Zealand. But the Hum in Taos was the most famous, and most studied, of them all. According to the latest statistics Chuck had read, around 2 percent of people who visited Taos could hear the strange noise; some found it so disconcerting they had to leave the town immediately, and others found it difficult to concentrate on anything other than the rumble as long as they could perceive it.

The Taos Hum was so well known, in fact, that by 1993, residents of New Mexico had joined together to petition the U.S. Congress to investigate. Theories were that the noise was related to nearby underground military installations or to the nuclear research going on in nearby Los Alamos. A university study was commissioned, but the scientists involved would eventually conclude that the phenomenon was not detectable by any scientific means. Still, stories of the Hum persisted, and Taos had landed on Chuck's travel wish list.

Tammy's father was a mechanical engineer, and he was intrigued by the possibility that something mechanical could be behind the phenomenon. That helped Chuck convince the rest of the family to detour off Interstate 40 toward Taos. Chuck himself favored an explanation involving an underground tunneling device; his fascination with Roswell and the way the military had gone to great lengths to cover up whatever had actually happened there had led him into many hours of tangential research into secret military bases. Area 51, Cheyenne Mountain, White Sands, Los Alamos—even the Pentagon—had vast, subterranean components. There could be networks of tunnels linking a number of these secret bases. Perhaps Taos was a weak point in that link, a spot along the surface just close enough to what was going on beneath that it affected a lucky few with the right sensitivity.

Unfortunately, no one in Chuck's family had been able to hear the Hum. The kids had had a good time kicking stones along a riverbank, Tammy had bought some American Indian artwork from a stand by the road, and Chuck's mother-in-law had probably wondered—for the hundredth time—about the seventeen-year-old boy who'd shown up to pick up her fifteen-year-old daughter for their first date wearing that red-white-and-blue motorcycle helmet from the movie *Easy Rider*, visor up, and knocked Tammy off her feet so far she was now riding around the American Southwest in an RV looking for UFOs.

Still, Chuck hadn't been discouraged. While the rest of the family had relaxed in the RV, he'd ventured out and talked with the local residents. He'd filled his notebook with information: that the Hum wasn't consistent; sometimes it could be heard all the time and other times not for weeks; the Hum had been going on for many years; and residents had even started to worry about their safety.

Afterward, he'd dropped off his in-laws at a golf resort in Albuquerque and had continued across the state with Tammy and the kids, accepting that most investigations—hell, maybe the vast majority of his investigations—were going to end similarly, with a lot of notes in a notebook, a lot of hearsay and conversations. Then again, he only needed to uncover real evidence, the sort that Tammy might accept, once. Even if 99.9 percent of the tens of thousands of UFO sightings over the years were mistakes, hoaxes, or hysteria, that still meant at least a few UFOs were real.

Of course, it wasn't UFOs or even the Taos Hum that had knocked the kids out to the point they could sleep through Chuck's handling of the jeep, as he navigated through the red-stone behemoths. For the two days since they'd hit Sedona, they'd been four-by-fouring these desolate, desert roads, visiting ancient Native American sites, climbing among the boulders, and speaking to the various natives they'd met along the route. Ashley had some pretty fragments of sandstone in a beaded leather pouch she'd bought at a reservation gift shop, while Chuck Jr. and Daniel had played cowboy among the more climbable rock formations. Chuck, always the tour guide, had tried to tell the boys that they were part of a long history of playing cowboy out here in Sedona; so many Hollywood Westerns had been filmed in the area because of the unique panoramas that you half expected John Wayne to step out from behind one of the monoliths.

Chuck himself had always felt more affinity with the Native Americans in those movies. Over the years, he'd visited several tribal reservations and had found that Native American culture seemed much more open to Chuck's fascination with the possibility of life on other worlds. A people who had lived under the stars, in touch with nature, Native Americans had never viewed the idea of UFOs or extraterrestrials as that big a deal. Nearly every tribe told stories of visitors from space. Shamans regularly communed with outer-worldly personalities and beings. The Anasazi of New Mexico had built solar observatories to track their star gods, and the Navajo told many stories of Skinwalkers—magical beings thought to have come from the stars, who had the ability to turn into animals. Certain places—often near reservations in Arizona, New Mexico, and Utah, many of which, Chuck had found, were also in areas where UFOs had been sighted—were known as hot spots for Skinwalkers, which landed them on Chuck's trip wish lists, though he hadn't checked any out yet. He'd read a bit about Skinwalker sightings near Dulce, New Mexico, that were supposedly associated with multiple UFO encounters, and he'd recently been reading about a ranch in Utah—known as Skinwalker Ranch. The ranch had such a rich history of terrifying sightings that two families had already moved out because of what they'd seen. Chuck didn't think Tammy was going to let him take the kids to New Mexico or Utah to meet Skinwalkers in person any time soon, but she certainly liked the kids' getting a familiarity with the Native American culture that had once dominated this part of the country.

And despite Hollywood's love for the location, the history of Sedona was more closely linked to Indians than cowboys. Aboriginal tribes had been living in the area since 11,000 BC. Paleo-era hunter-gatherers had given way to Yavapai nomads, switching off with various tribes until the Apache had moved in around the middle of the fifteenth century. In 1876, most of the remaining Apaches had been force-marched to a camp in San Carlos, 180 miles away. The few who survived the long walk through the desert were interned there for years, before being shuttled off to various reservations.

Descendants of the Apaches, after eventually making their way back to Sedona, had first spoken of an energy vortex, the phenomenon that had put the location on Chuck's trip list.

"Another mile, maybe two," Chuck said to Tammy, with a gesture toward the brochure. "We should catch sight of Bell Rock in a few minutes."

Tammy didn't answer, but Chuck could tell by the expression on her face that she was ready to head back to the campsite where the RV was parked, or at the very least, join the kids in the backseat. So far, the trip to Sedona had been much like Taos; they'd made two stops at sites notorious for viewing a vortex—the Airport Road Vortex and the Cathedral Rock Vortex—where they'd gotten out, walked around a bit, then gotten back in the jeep. After that Tammy fully expected Bell Rock to be strike three. But Chuck wasn't discouraged. He'd had a chance to talk to a half dozen Native Americans who lived in the area, and had filled three pages with notes of what it was like to experience a vortex. As in Taos, he felt certain he was documenting something real. Whether there was a link to UFOs or whether it was just some sort of natural phenomenon, he couldn't say. But there was something going on here.

"You sure these things come out at night?"

Chuck didn't answer right away; the truth was, he knew fairly little about how vortices were supposed to work, other than what Tammy had also read in the brochure. Even in the weeks leading up to the trip, he'd found precious little about them beyond the barest descriptions. Supposedly, Sedona had numerous hot spots where vortices appeared, resembling electrically charged tornadoes that spiraled up and down with spiritual energy. The Native Americans would use these specific locations to communicate with spiritual beings, and to commune with their ancestors in the stars.

"From the stories I've heard," he said, "it isn't something you can even see. It just overwhelms you . . ."

Chuck stopped midsentence. Without warning, the jeep's headlights blinked off and lights on the road ahead suddenly went out. Everything was pitch-black. Chuck stared down at the dashboard. The vehicle had somehow just died. No engine, no headlights, no taillights, nothing on the dash. Everything was out. The jeep continued to roll forward, but everything powered by electricity was gone.

"Chuck?"

"I don't know. It just stopped."

"What do you mean, it stopped?"

Chuck grabbed at the key, which was still in the ignition, and began jiggling it—still nothing. He looked around and through the windows, but could see only the ambient light from the stars and the Moon. Nobody else was on the road ahead or behind them. It was just them, in the dead jeep, rolling along in near silence.

Chuck pulled hard at the wheel, since the automatic steering was gone, coaxing the vehicle toward the side of the road. It gradually slowed to a stop, two wheels in the sand.

"This is a joke, right? You're playing a joke."

Tammy had half a smile on her face. She really did think Chuck was toying with her. She knew from the many stories Chuck had told her that in a large number of UFO sightings, vehicles would lose power, batteries would die: She assumed this was just Chuck trying to scare the hell out of her. But when she could see through the darkness to make out the look in Chuck's eyes, her smile vanished, replaced by panic. She glanced back at the kids, who were still fast asleep.

"Chuck," she said, quietly.

"I gotta go check this out," he responded, reaching for the door handle. But Tammy grabbed his other arm, her fingers so tight he could feel her nails through his shirt.

"You stay in this car."

Chuck had already pushed the door a few inches open, but Tammy didn't let go. She hadn't held on to him that tightly since their wedding dance. Every beat of Chuck's heart was pushing him to climb out of that jeep. They were in an area known for strange energy vortices that Native Americans believed had links to the stars. The chance of Chuck's actually seeing a UFO had never been higher. But he stopped himself. Sitting in silence, Tammy's fingers against his arm, he could hear the kids' cadenced breathing from the backseat. He slowly shut the jeep door.

Just as the door clicked back into place, the headlights blinked on, so bright Chuck had to close his eyes. When he opened them, the dashboard was lit up as if nothing had ever happened. The engine growled to life, the taillights flickered on, and Tammy finally released her grip, her eyes darting back and forth, checking out the desert around them, then the kids, then the desert again.

Nothing. Just sand, road, and the sandstone rocks, looming frozen in place as they'd been for thousands of years.

"Was that a vortex?" Tammy asked.

What had just happened wasn't at all what the witnesses Chuck interviewed had described; it was something much closer to what happened near a UFO sighting. His scientific mind took over, going through the facts. The jeep was brand new, rented just a couple of days earlier, and had very few miles on it. They had been four-by-fouring all day on rough roads and trails, and had never experienced any problems. There was no smell of electrical burning or any signs of engine damage that Chuck could detect—other than that the engine had just completely cut out on him. The vehicle seemed perfectly fine, as it had been since they'd rented the thing.

Chuck had given in to Tammy and the priorities in his life, the safety of his family, and stayed in the car. Even though he didn't really think there would have been any risk in stepping out, he hadn't been willing to take that chance. Deep down, he wasn't sure he'd always have that sort of self-control.

"I think maybe it's time we head back to the campsite," Tammy said. "That's about as much spirituality as I can take in one night."

Chuck could tell from the change in her voice that she'd already started to doubt what she'd just witnessed. Her mind was analyzing the moment and edging back toward a rational interpretation. Chuck was a believer: To him, a brand-new jeep didn't die in the middle of the road in a place like Sedona without cause. But he had no evidence that it was due to an extraordinary cause, so he wasn't going to convince Tammy that it was.

Just a dead jeep, a believer and his skeptical wife, a trio of sleeping kids, on a road in the desert.

# CHAPTER 8

## NATIONAL ATOMIC MUSEUM,
## ALBUQUERQUE, NEW MEXICO,
## JULY 1996

Amodern city skyline, maybe New York, maybe Los Angeles, maybe Houston, Miami, or Washington. A frozen moment, a steel and concrete pincushion set against a cloudless blue sky, like an image painted across a pane of glass. And then, right above the tallest spire, a flash of light, so intense it seemed to crack the very sky. A second later, an enormous fireball, rising upward: And then everything caught fire, the buildings, the asphalt streets, even the air. A few seconds later a concussive wave hit, an invisible sphere shattering everything in its path. Metal and cinder block crashed outward, wood and glass instantly disintegrating. After the shock wave, the wind—over three hundred miles per hour—radiated outward in every direction. The fireball still rose, gathering particles, pulling inward like a vacuum, creating the classic mushroom cloud. But by then the entire city was engulfed in a firestorm that seemed both biblical and science fiction, the joining of shared, primitive fears and futuristic nightmares.

*Incredible.* Chuck was close enough to the video monitor to see his own reflection in the screen, dancing above the billowing clouds of flame. His three kids were lined up along the railing to his right, wide-eyed as they watched along with him. Tammy was nearby, leafing through some of the other objects in the exhibit; Chuck had a feeling she was less intrigued by the awesome power of the nuclear test explosion on the TV, and more concerned about the call they would probably get the first day the kids eventually headed back to school. Maybe taking the kids to learn about the history of atomic warfare wasn't the best way to spend a day smack in the middle of summer vacation, but Chuck hadn't been able to help himself.

After Taos and Sedona, they were back in Albuquerque to pick up Tammy's parents, and Chuck had figured, what better way to end a road trip than a quick stop at the National Atomic Museum, located on Kirkland Air Force Base near the outskirts of the city.

The two boys had been thrilled with the idea; what twelve-year-old didn't want to learn about big, destructive bombs. And Ashley might still have been too young to understand what she was seeing, but she was happy to show to her stuffed alien, Mr. Chalupa, the various historic paraphernalia, including actual casings of the two bombs that had been dropped in Japan at the end of World War II, Little Boy and Fat Man.

Chuck wasn't nearly as interested in the bombs themselves or the massive scenes of destruction they were capable of creating as he was fascinated by the enormous, secret engineering effort that had led to their development, and especially the unprecedented scale of what was known as the Manhattan Project.

Coming from a military family—his father was a decorated soldier and tank specialist in World War II and Korea—Chuck had never believed that the government was particularly capable of covering things up, so he wasn't a conspiracy theorist. In CIA operations, from the assassination attempts against Castro to the various sorties involving terrorist organizations, there was almost always evidence left behind: a crashed helicopter, bullet casings, eyewitnesses.

Roswell was a perfect example. So many eyewitnesses: Glenn Dennis, the mortician who had delivered child-sized coffins; Jesse Marcel and his son, Jesse Marcel, Jr., who had personally handled the UFO debris; Mac Brazel, the rancher, and his neighbor who had helped cart the material off the field. Hell, Chuck hoped one day to get the chance to visit the crash site himself, because he felt sure that no matter how hard the air force had tried to vacuum up all the hard evidence, something would have been left behind. Something was always left behind.

But the Manhattan Project had been different. A massive, secret project that had involved more than 130,000 people, it had cost more than twenty-six billion in current dollars. It was a project that had included the creation from scratch of whole towns, such as Los Alamos, Hanford, and Oak Ridge—the last a municipality in Tennessee that itself became known as the Secret City, a sixty-thousand-acre village surrounded by guard towers and fences, with a population in the thousands, none of whom had any idea what the real purpose of their community might have been. This had been a true conspiracy on the highest level.

Of the 130,000 people involved in creating the atom bomb, maybe two dozen had actually known the details of the entire project. It wasn't until Little Boy and Fat Man were dropped on Hiroshima and Nagasaki that most of the people who had been a part of the Manhattan Project realized what they had been building.

If a government that wasn't very good at keeping secrets had been able to keep such a mammoth undertaking covert enough to surprise even the people on the inside, who knew what else it was capable of? The Manhattan Project had taken place between 1942 and 1946, and a year later, Roswell happened. The same machinery that had kept the development of nuclear weapons clandestine had still been in place when something had hit the ground on that ranch, right near the very air force base where the B-29s that had carried Little Boy and Fat Man had been housed.

That had been only the beginning. The relationship between UFO sightings and nuclear bases was well documented. Chuck had an entire section of his file cabinet dedicated to sightings near bases, including the famous story of craft spotted and tracked by radar over Malmstrom Air Force Base in Montana in 1967, witnessed by base security officers and nuclear engineers, and the unexplained, sudden shutdown of at least ten ICBM missiles housed in silos beneath the UFO activity. Los Alamos, where the atomic bombs were first designed, had sightings going back even further, to 1948, two years after the end of the Manhattan Project, that were reportedly documented in FBI files, since liberally redacted and designated as top secret. Chuck had seen some of those files; a few were so heavily redacted that the pages were mostly black ink. One line he'd read over and over again had been indicative of the beloved military tactic: "███████ unidentified objects ███████ not ███████."

Whatever had originally been written in that file had been blacked out to the point that it could have been communicating almost anything. It might very well have seemed more suspicious because of the redacting than it would have been if it had been left alone.

He'd regaled Tammy and the kids about the UFO-nuke connection on the drive over to the museum; as usual, it had been a hard sell. The idea that aliens might be benevolent enough to watch over the developing nuclear program in the forties, fifties, and sixties seemed far-fetched and Hollywood. Likewise, the thought that nuclear weapons were some sort of calling card to UFOs—some technological checkpoint or red flag—seemed a mix of hubris and science fiction. A skeptic might point out that nuclear weapons, developed in secret, would be particularly interesting to foreign governments, as well as competing domestic secret services. Observation craft, or even primitive drones and the U-2s designed at Area 51, would certainly appear like UFOs. And who knew what the Russians had been developing at the time or what else Area 51 had cooked up?

Whatever the connection between UFOs and nukes might be, there was no arguing with the fact that cover-ups did exist. The people behind the Manhattan Project had covered up an entire town, and they hadn't stopped there.

As the fireball subsided and the video screen went blank, Chuck found himself staring at his own reflection, so he followed Tammy and the kids into an adjoining room in the interior of the museum—a small theater, lined with polyester-clad seats in front of a pull-down screen. He sat between Tammy and Ashley, Mr. Chalupa bouncing up and down against his knee.

When the room went dark, Chuck settled in to watch a black-and-white film, a documentary about the Manhattan Project from beginning to end. The first few minutes lulled him and he nearly dozed off, but he perked up as the film shifted into a discussion of the great lengths to which the people running the project had gone in order to try to maintain secrecy. According to the film, the Office of Censorship, created in 1941, had actually taken words out of the English language to help keep the project secret; words like "atomic" and "nuclear" were pulled from newspapers and magazines, even comic books. When the narrator of the film boasted that the agency had censored the popular comic *Buck Rogers*, Chuck figured he finally had some evidence to show Tammy that the government really did have the capability to censor any level of media. But glancing past his kids to where Tammy was seated, he saw she'd fallen asleep.

More irony: Here he was, watching a government-sponsored film that proudly detailed the mechanisms behind a secret conspiracy.

And Tammy simply closed her eyes.

# CHAPTER 9

## LAS VEGAS, NEVADA,
## EIGHTY MILES WEST OF AREA 51,
## SPRING 1953

37.2350° N, 115.8111° W

A little before 5:00 a.m., nine-year-old Robert Bigelow* was only half-way asleep, but something was waking him up fast. His eyes were still somewhere between open and closed, his mop of brownish-blond hair sticking up from his head in random sprouts like some sort of demented halo. He got both legs over the edge of the bed, the covers still clinging to his pajama-clad body, then his bare feet hit the floor and he was diving forward across his bedroom toward the window, nearly upending a huge stack of *Buck Rogers* comic books as he went. He slipped just as he reached the other side of the room, barely catching himself on the jutting wooden windowsill, his fingernails sending a rain of chipped paint to the hard wooden floorboards. He reached for the bottom of the shade, giving it enough of a yank to send the thin white sheet of canvas rolling toward the ceiling. His

---

* Though I was not able to interview Robert Bigelow by the time this volume went to press, my account of his thoughts is drawn from extensive research and secondary sources as referenced in the bibliography, including multiple interviews that he has given in the past.

face was right up against the glass, eyes now fully wide, the last vestiges of sleep racing out of him with each pound of his heart against his chest.

*My god.* A mushroom cloud was rising like some sort of billowing jelly-fish above the horizon. Even eighty miles away, it was clearly visible—partly because there wasn't much to get in the way. The city of Las Vegas itself was just getting its footing—the newly opened Sahara and Sands christening the Strip, adding to the constant neon haze rising from Fremont Street downtown. But beyond the under-construction city limits, there was just about nothing and nobody. Vast tracts of desert, crags, and hills, lots of brush, and dried-up lakes and riverbeds. It was the reason the military had chosen the area in the first place; lucky coincidence had given Bigelow a front-row seat.

He figured it was the shock wave that had first awakened him. Even now, maybe a full minute past detonation, his bedroom was still shaking, the high shelves along the wall behind his bed threatening to spill their contents—more comic books, plastic toy robots, and green army men—all over the floor. Hell, the whole house felt as if it was lurching up and down, from the foundation on up. In fact, he was pretty sure the whole damn town was shaking.

Bigelow had read in the newspapers that sometimes, when the bombs at the nearby National Atomic Testing Site were particularly big, even downtown Vegas got seismic readings on par with low-level earthquakes. He reached forward, spreading his palms against the glass pane. He wasn't certain, but he thought he could actually feel the heat emanating from the blast, even eighty miles away. So much raw power—it seemed unworldly, even though it was entirely of this world.

He had seen the mushroom clouds many times before. From his bedroom, from his backyard, sometimes eating breakfast in his kitchen downstairs, even at school. Once in a while they released class early so the students could go out on the playground and watch the bombs—Bigelow had cheered right along with his classmates when the mushroom clouds went up, up, up. According to the newspapers, it was a tourist draw on par with the casinos.

Unlike with the Manhattan Project, there was nothing secret about what Bigelow was witnessing. Hell, it was quite the opposite. Since Hiroshima and Nagasaki, Nellis Air Force Base and the National Atomic Testing Site had become known throughout the country as ground zero of the nation's atomic future. In fact, before the first set of test detonations, the military had even put up flyers, all over town:

# WARNING

January 11, 1951

From this day forward the U. S. Atomic Energy Commission has been authorized to use part of the Las Vegas Bombing and Gunnery Range for test work necessary to the atomic weapons development program.

Test activities will include experimental nuclear detonations for the development of atomic bombs — so-called "A-Bombs" — carried out under controlled conditions.

Tests will be conducted on a routine basis for an indefinite period.

## NO PUBLIC ANNOUNCEMENT OF THE TIME OF ANY TEST WILL BE MADE

Unauthorized persons who pass inside the limits of the Las Vegas Bombing and Gunnery Range may be subject to injury from or as a result of the AEC test activities.

Health and safety authorities have determined that no danger from or as a result of AEC test activities may be expected outside the limits of the Las Vegas Bombing and Gunnery Range. All necessary precautions, including radiological surveys and patrolling of the surrounding territory, will be undertaken to insure that safety conditions are maintained.

Full security restrictions of the Atomic Energy Act will apply to the work in this area.

RALPH P. JOHNSON, Project Manager
Las Vegas Project Office
U. S. Atomic Energy Commission

Growing up in a place like Las Vegas, Bigelow was used to seeing strange things. Heck, the city itself was strange; from the giant neon cowboy that stood over Fremont Street to the Rat Pack–inspired night owls who were now hitting the Strip, hoping to brush elbows with movie stars and mobsters who dressed like movie stars. But what went on out there in the desert—the mushroom clouds were just the most visible manifestation of the machinery beneath, the one-eighth of an iceberg that floated above the surface. The other seven-eighths was concealed in tunnels and bunkers, behind code names and within the blacked-out boxes— ██████████ —of redacted files.

Bigelow was just a kid, not even ten, but already he'd developed a fascination with the unknown, the hidden conspiracies and shadows that lurked out there, beneath the mushroom clouds. He wasn't like his classmates—he'd taken to thoughts of futuristic technology and secret science the way other kids took to baseball, dinosaurs, and race cars. He'd read everything he could find, newspapers, library books, even comic books, and had asked every adult who'd take him seriously about the stories he had heard. Most of all, he always kept his eyes open. Living in Nevada, you saw things the rest of the world knew nothing about. Nellis Air Force Base was just one part of a much larger military zone that contained both the nuclear test site and at least one experimental flight base.

He might not have ever heard the name Area 51, which was mentioned in military documents, even in passing, until a long-gestating FOIA request was finally unsealed in 2013. But he could certainly fantasize about the wild spy planes that were being developed and tested there, planes that could fly at seventy-five thousand feet, nearly invisible to modern radar. Or the even stranger craft that might have come out of earlier war efforts and the rapidly developing Cold War.

Fantasies aside, he did know for certain that if you watched the night sky, especially in the direction of the nuclear testing site, you would occasionally see things that didn't make sense. Eerie, glowing red objects that appeared to be flying in formation. Dark, triangular craft that seemed to hover, then glide.

The mushroom clouds, the spy planes—these were advanced, but man-made. But the other flying objects—these were harder to explain. Bigelow had spent much of his childhood hearing stories from neighbors and family members, and he knew he was not alone in his suspicions. People who grew up where he was growing up spent a lot of time thinking about UFOs. The event at Roswell and the hysteria around the multitudes of reports of flying saucers were a constant refrain in Nevada. For Bigelow, these were more than just campfire stories. He was obsessed with the idea of space, of visitors from the stars. More than that, witnessing the incredible scientific achievements, secret or not, out there in the desert had inspired him to think of space as a two-way highway. One day, he believed, humanity would find a way to travel to the stars and beyond. At nine years old, Bigelow dreamed of being part of that accomplishment.

Even at his young age, he knew the only real obstacle to those dreams of space would be money; the military bases out in the desert had cost the government billions, and getting to space would no doubt be equally expensive. Bigelow was just a kid, and his family wasn't rich. But he was determined; somehow, one day, he was going to be part of the race to see what was out there, beyond the stars. And if he was right—that whatever was out there had already visited *here*—he intended to plunge himself into that story as well.

# CHAPTER 10

"You know, some husbands send flowers. Roses are nice, violets, too. And chocolate. I've heard that some husbands give chocolate."

Tammy pushed an errant lock of hair out of her eyes with her gloved right hand, leaving a trail of reddish mud across her forehead. With her other hand, she carefully shook a steel sifting pan over the aluminum tray that sat in the dirt between them.

"Or a nice dinner at a restaurant. It doesn't even have to be that expensive. I'd take an Olive Garden. At least you don't spend two days doing laundry after a visit to the Olive Garden."

Chuck was glad their instructor—an associate professor of archaeology moonlighting from the University of Tucson—had wandered off on some errand, leaving them alone in the dig pit. The young man might have misconstrued Tammy's comments and the anguished expression on her face. Perhaps he'd even have thought that she was less than thrilled about spending her fifteenth wedding anniversary on her hands and knees in an excavation pit, digging through the entrance to a prehistoric Anasazi pueblo, looking for broken pieces of pottery in thousand-year-old mud.

64

But Chuck could tell by the spark in Tammy's eyes that she was enjoying the experience almost as much as he was. It helped that after just a little over two days at the Raven Archeology Ruin Site, she'd already become the star pupil; sifting through remnants of the pueblo at a spot a few ruined chambers over, she had uncovered a wooden support strut, shutting down the entire dig so that the archaeologists could analyze her discovery. The strut, it turned out, was evidence of a second story that the Raven experts hadn't accounted for, winning Tammy prize status among the handful of students who had signed up for the course on an off-season May weekend, and more important, giving Tammy endless bragging rights over Chuck. He was the big-shot investigator who had somehow convinced her that a weekend learning how to properly curate, restore, and preserve specimens from a prehistoric dig—or, say, a less prehistoric UFO crash site—could be just as romantic as dinner and chocolates.

"Speak for yourself," Chuck responded, gingerly lifting a small piece of material that could have been a seashell—a form of currency among the primitive Native American tribes—between his gloved fingers. "When I go to the Olive Garden there tends to be plenty of laundry to do the next day. You've seen me eat."

Tammy rolled her eyes and sifted a little more sand, her movements careful and determined. He was impressed at how she'd thrown herself into the lessons; willingness to support him in his crazy passion-quest was one thing, but being game enough to take an archaeology course at a pueblo dig site in Arizona, that was above and beyond.

Actually, it was Tammy who had found a brochure to the Raven site on a rack at a hole-in-the-wall motel they had stayed at six weeks earlier; Chuck had been out in the nearby forest, checking out a supposed sighting—a pair of hunters had reported seeing a cigar-shaped flying object rising above the trees, and their believability factor had been high enough to get their picture in the local town paper. While the kids had blinked their way through the heavily chlorinated water in the motel's kidney-shaped swimming pool, Tammy had read enough of the pamphlet to realize it was something Chuck was going to jump at:

She probably hadn't expected him to plan the trip for their anniversary, but then again, she'd often complained that his beliefs and her skepticism created a sort of wall, or maybe more accurately, a divide when it came to his passion. Joining him in UFO investigations in the field seemed too dangerous—and, frankly, her unwillingness to take anything at face value often sent him on a rant. But archaeology was something scientific, something they could learn together.

Tammy's enthusiasm had only bolstered Chuck's conviction that it was just this sort of scientific education that he needed to pursue; more and more, he was taking his investigations seriously, and more and more, *he* wanted to be taken seriously. Having Tammy as a foil only showed him how much more precise and analytical he needed to be. If she could easily discount what he considered "evidence," then it wasn't evidence at all. Two hunters who said they saw something in the forest meant very little to Tammy, but a wooden beam in a primitive pueblo was enough to shut down an archaeological dig.

Chuck understood the difference between this sort of science and hearsay. His day job engineering microchips relied entirely on math and rationality; there was no room for anything that didn't have a logical foundation. He needed to approach his investigations in the same way.

From all the reading he had done, and all the conferences he had attended—MUFON and otherwise—he had discovered that there was a huge lack of scientific expertise in the UFO field. It was partially for this reason that it was so easy for the world to discount the possibility of UFOs, despite so much first-person reportage. Without any real science to back up the sightings, it was just so many hunters out in the woods telling stories.

Chuck didn't know for certain how, but he believed that the skills he was learning at the Raven site would help him in the future. From the minute they'd arrived at the grounds of the pueblo dig, he had thrown himself into learning everything he could about the process behind uncovering materials, no matter how long they had been buried.

Because it was the middle of May and not really the summer tourist season yet, he and Tammy had the run of the site. The normal procedure for the course was to be introduced to the excavation of a ruin site, then absorb lessons on curation techniques and restoration, basically putting pieces of found pottery together like a puzzle. But the lack of other students meant Chuck and Tammy could concentrate on the excavation and focus on archaeological dig techniques.

Over the past few days, he and Tammy had become near experts on "strip" digging, which was basically digging level by level, in very thin strips, from the surface downward. Depending on the type of rock or mud at the site, very few centimeters translated to hundreds of years, which meant you didn't need to go that deep to go back a fair amount of time. Considering the type of research Chuck knew he would be conducting in the future, it was important for him to become adept at figuring out not just where he was looking, but when. Sifting through the reddish mud almost felt like time travel, and the more controlled he could become at the effort, the more finely tuned his time machine.

"It's amazing to think that this seashell—if it really is a seashell—might have been dropped by some Anasazi trader, maybe six hundred years ago. A tribe that just plain disappeared in the sixteenth century—nobody knows why—and we're looking at a piece of evidence that at least one minute of one day, they were right here."

Tammy had heard plenty about the Anasazi over the years. Not only had the primitive tribe vanished mysteriously, but they had been surprisingly advanced astronomers, leaving behind evidence of amazingly accurate solar observatories. They'd also left multistoried pueblos and dwellings, carved so high up in cliff faces that another mystery was how they got in and out, let alone constructed such complex edifices. One theory was that the way they built their homes, terrifyingly high up in the cliffs, was linked to the way they had mysteriously disappeared—that they were trying to hide, or avoid some sort of fatal threat—one that eventually caught up with them.

"Chuck, no matter how much they loved the stars, the Anasazi were Native Americans, not aliens."

"Doesn't mean they didn't have friends in high places."

Chuck was mostly joking. He was willing to believe that the Egyptian pyramids, Native American wall paintings depicting star travelers, and odd South American rock formations had parallels to modern UFO sightings, but he hadn't read much about them because he had no way of personally investigating them. He did know a bit about Native American mythology—and that much of it seemed to reference extraterrestrial phenomena. For instance, the Apache referred to their ancestors as "Star People," pale, white, skinny humanoids with blue eyes who traveled in craft described as "birds with many colors" that "glowed with the sun." But that was where his expertise on the subject ended; he had three kids and an RV, not a team of history professors and archaeologists. He was on his own with his abilities as a "talker" to learn whatever he could from the people he met. And he had his notebooks and filing cabinets.

The more he filled the notebooks, the more he believed that it was all leading toward a significant shift in the direction his life was taking. Even the littlest addition—a seashell caught in a sifter full of dirt—was pushing him forward. He'd shared his premonitions with Tammy many times, but she'd mostly written them off as the sort of musings she'd heard before.

"If they really had friends in high places," Tammy said, "I don't think the only thing left of their culture would be five-hundred-year-old buried ruins, to be picked through by weekenders looking for seashells."

She placed her sifter on the ground by her knees and reached for the water bottle Velcroed to their nearby gear. Chuck continued examining the object in his hands, finally deciding that it wasn't, in fact, a seashell, but more likely a chipped piece of stone left behind by a less careful first-time archaeology student.

A moment ago, he'd thought he was holding a symbol of an entire lost civilization, and now there was nothing in his hand but a meaningless bit of rock. *Supposition and belief, countered by scientific observation.* The first half came naturally to him—the second, more important part was what he needed to master.

He tossed the chip into the mud and went back to his sifter.

# CHAPTER 11

*B*reathe in. Breathe out.

Chuck focused on the two inches of sunlight fighting through the bottom of the drawn window shade directly across the stark, cubic interrogation room, trying his best to keep his heart rate normal.

*Breathe in. Breathe out.*

The skin of his right arm whitened as the blood-pressure cuff constricted; meanwhile, the wires running from his chest and the straps around each finger—spread out flat against the cold wood of the police sergeant's desk—of his left hand waved in the breeze from the overtaxed air conditioners. *Mid-November, and the damn place feels like an icebox.* Even so, beads of sweat ran down the back of Chuck's neck.

*Breathe in.*

The police officer on the other side of the desk checked the monitor attached to the wires, then leaned toward Chuck and asked the question a second time: "Have you ever been accused or convicted of a crime, and do you know of any police records or files pertaining to you?"

*Breathe out . . .*

Chuck closed his eyes. It was no use. He wasn't sure whether his answer was going to be the truth or a lie, and either way, he was so nervous he was going to set the machine off and ruin his chances of getting into the department—and blow three months of the hardest work he'd ever done training at the Sheriff's Citizens' Academy.

Crazy that it was the polygraph that was going to break him, after everything he'd gone through to get into that interrogation room. Even though the reserve program was strictly voluntary, the training was the same as if Chuck were entering the police force as a full officer. He'd passed the difficult written test to enter the Deputy Reserves—a test that more than 70 percent of candidates failed. He also passed the psych eval with flying colors, surprising himself and Tammy, who had clearly felt he was going to bomb. Then he'd submitted to months of physical training and more testing, as well as performance ratings and firearms guidance. If he finally earned a uniform, he would have the exact same responsibilities as a full-time paid deputy. Even the uniforms were the same, except for a smaller patch above the larger sheriff's shoulder patch that said "Reserve."

But now gaining that uniform seemed as remote as when he'd started the program, all because of the polygraph, the last step in the ordeal before the tribunal and board certification. When he'd first made the decision to become a sheriff's deputy, he'd never imagined that something as simple as a lie detector could derail his plans.

Selling Tammy on the idea of the move to Colorado Springs had been difficult; her family was in California, where they'd both grown up, and she'd had a comfortable job in shipping at a major airline based outside San Diego. Chuck's job at the microchip firm in California had likewise offered stability and advancement opportunities, but increasingly, the strict hours and structured work environment had made it difficult for him to conduct his UFO investigations in the way he felt was necessary. Often, he'd get a call of a sighting, but by the time he could get off work, get into the jeep or the RV, and head out into the field to question witnesses and find evidence, any traces of what had happened had disappeared. He needed a job with a little more flexibility if he was going to delve deeper into his research.

More and more often, Chuck had found himself heading in the direction of the mountains. For whatever reason, the UFO sightings he was hearing about seemed to happen more often in the middle of the country: Nevada, Arizona, Utah, and Colorado. Weekend after weekend, with or without the family, he'd found himself driving hundreds of miles to investigate reports. After a dozen Colorado incidents, he'd started to build a network of UFO buffs in the area, and through his conversations with these like-minded sources, he'd started to get curious about cattle and animal mutilations. This UFO-related phenomenon was new—to him. Though in 1998 he was far from an expert in the field, he'd already learned enough to know that these incidents were serious, pervasive, and poorly investigated. In order to learn more, he added thousands of road miles to his journeys. Colorado turned out to be the hotbed of animal mutilations, with dozens being reported every month.

Chuck felt himself pulled toward the state. A few phone calls led to an offer of a job at a microchip firm in Colorado Springs, Atmel Micro-Controller Company, and he'd jumped at the opportunity. As a senior design engineer, he was still going to have trouble getting free to conduct his investigations, but at least he'd be closer to where the incidents occurred, and he'd have a chance to delve into them firsthand. Tammy had finally acquiesced. The air was good, the community was child-friendly and healthy, and the mountains were spectacular. She wasn't thrilled with what Chuck was finding on the ranches in the shadows of those beautiful peaks, but she was always supportive.

Six months after their move, Chuck learned about the Sheriff's Citizens' Academy and the Deputy Reserves. Coming from a military family, he'd always been interested in law enforcement, and here was a chance to get involved with the department—get a uniform, a badge, and a gun—while still keeping his day job. He also figured that joining the police force might get him quicker access to the sort of incident reports that he'd been investigating on his own. He was certain that law enforcement was seeing things that weren't getting out to the public. When a UFO was spotted in the sky or a head of cattle was mutilated on a ranch, the first thing a rancher did was call the police. The story didn't make it into the newspapers or onto TV until well after the sheriff's department investigated the incident, often trampling over the best evidence in their efforts to find something mundane in the remarkable. If Chuck became a deputy, maybe once in a while he'd be the first person on the scene.

The three-month Citizens' Academy training course had been difficult—filling his nights and weekends—but Chuck had loved the physical aspects of the job, and he had quickly made friends throughout the department. The first driver's training class had been an experience all its own. Cones had been set up all over a minor league baseball stadium parking lot for the trainees to learn maneuvers like swerving, backing up, and other high-speed chase scenarios. One of the patrol cars had been parked on the other end of the lot, and the instructor had asked Chuck to go retrieve it for the lesson.

Stepping into the cop car, flipping on the lights, Chuck had felt such a thrill that he had immediately called Tammy on his cell phone. When the instructor began waving at him to hurry the hell up, he had immediately put the car into reverse—and found himself flashing back to his high school years with his 1970 Ford Mustang stick shift. He'd gone right into what he and his motorhead friends had called "The Rockford Maneuver," taken from their favorite TV show, *The Rockford Files*. He'd slammed his foot against the gas pedal, tearing backward across the parking lot, then tapped the brakes and yanked the wheel to the left, whipping the car into a 180-degree skid. Straightening out, he'd driven over to the instructor and put the car into park.

The minute he'd gotten out, he saw red cauliflowers exploding across the training officer's cheeks.

"Was that an authorized training maneuver?" the man had shouted, while the other trainees had fought back laughter. Still, Chuck had managed to pass the vehicle course with flying colors. In fact, he'd gotten through all the training without much trouble. He had already begun imagining himself out on the highway in a patrol car.

Then came the polygraph. He'd done his best to prepare himself the night before, going over the likely questions with Tammy, trying to calm his nerves at the thought of being attached to a machine that reflected his inner thoughts by measuring his outer physical cues: heart rate, breathing, and temperature. All he had to do to beat the machine and pass the test was tell the truth.

"Have you ever been accused or convicted of a crime, and do you know of any police records or files pertaining to you?"

He decided to level with the officer.

"Well, there's Roswell. And the Area 51 incident. But I'm not sure those count."

The officer stared at him, then repeated, "Roswell. Area 51."

"Right. Roswell, in Nevada. In 1947 a UFO supposedly crashed . . ."

"I know what Roswell is, Mr. Zukowski. Would you mind explaining what the hell you are talking about?"

So Chuck dived into his story. Since the first family trip to Roswell, he'd gone back numerous times, usually on his own. The kids had gotten sick of listening to him interview everyone he came across, and there were only so many times they found it fun to eat at the Crashdown Café, a UFO-themed diner that had been open fairly continuously since Mac Brazel had found that strange debris on his ranch. By '98, Chuck had been to Roswell so often, he'd become a fixture in the UFO Museum. He had become friendly with Glenn Dennis, and he'd also gotten to know many other first-person witnesses to the event, including Walter Haut, the public information officer who had put out the air force's initial flying saucer press release, and Julie Schuster, the daughter of a witness to the overflight of the supposed UFO. His repeated meetings with these sources had increased his appetite to learn more about the crash, and he'd spent many hours circling the old, fenced-off air force base nearby.

He'd spent many late nights sitting in his darkened jeep outside the fence, watching the empty warehouses. And on one of those nights, he'd first noticed an unmarked SUV parked on the edge of the highway just a dozen yards from where he was sitting. When he'd started up the jeep to head back to the RV campground where he'd left his own Winnebago, the SUV had turned on its lights as well, following him for the first few miles, then turning away, heading off into the darkness.

In the beginning, Chuck had thought nothing of it. Just a fellow UFO lover, tracing the same steps that had led Chuck to stare at warehouses in the middle of night. It wasn't until Chuck's first visit to Area 51 that he realized that something more might be going on.

Although precious little had ever been published about Area 51—most of it just supposition and fantasy—Chuck believed that there were connections between Roswell and a secret military base. At the very least, whatever had crashed at Roswell was reportedly taken to Area 51.

Access to the base itself was impossible, and highly illegal. The best a tourist could do was to trek up one of the nearby rises and hope for a glimpse beyond the high fences and military barricades. Chuck had heard that the military had recently closed down the most famous viewing spot—Freedom Ridge, a jutting, rocky crag atop a winding brush trail, about twelve miles from the base itself—but there was another nearby ridge with a good view of the action called Tikaboo Peak that industrious tour guides had recently discovered. Chuck had made the necessary arrangements to hire one of the guides for what he thought was going to be a private tour, and had headed to the parking area to meet him for the trek up the side of the cliff.

To his surprise, the guide had arrived accompanied by a pair of strangers. One had seemed obviously military to Chuck, with well-coiffed hair and wearing fatigues. The second had seemed more surfer than military, but from the start both men had seemed to be suspiciously interested in Chuck's history, asking a lot of questions about his past, his interest in UFOlogy, and his reasons for wanting to see Area 51.

When they'd reached the viewing summit, the men had seemed much more interested in watching Chuck than anything that was going on in the military base. At first, there hadn't been too much to see down below, even through a pair of high-powered binoculars—just an expanse of fenced-off desert and a few squat buildings that could have been warehouses. But then at one point, an area of the ground in the center of one of the fences had slid open to reveal a ramp leading underground. Two military trucks covered in tarps had emerged, then the ground had closed up behind them, and the trucks had driven off past the farthest blocky buildings. Chuck had been excited by the sight, trying to imagine what sort of underground complex might have been buried out there in the desert—but when he'd turned back toward his companions, he saw the guy who looked like military shoving what appeared to be a palm-sized camera into the pocket of his fatigues. Chuck couldn't be sure, but he thought the man had just taken his picture.

Upon their return from Tikaboo, the two men had climbed into a dark-windowed SUV. Chuck had been too suspicious of the men to let it end like that, so he'd followed in his jeep, keeping a healthy few cars' distance between them, until they'd reached a nearby campground. The SUV had stopped next to a camper-trailer, and one of the men had gone inside. Then the SUV had driven off.

Chuck had waited five minutes, then exited his truck and approached the trailer. He knocked on the aluminum siding three times. The military guy opened the door and stood there, staring at him. Chuck glanced past him into the trailer, where a laptop lay open on the floor and a green military duffel bag rested on a sheetless bed. Other than that, the interior of the trailer was completely empty. Not even a coffeepot or an extra set of clothes.

Chuck looked back to the man, who was still staring at him, face devoid of expression. Then Chuck said the only thing he could think to say.

"I'm no threat, am I?"

The man had continued to look at him silently and then he'd slowly smiled.

"Yeah, you're no threat. You're just a UFO nut."

The man closed the trailer door and Chuck drove away. The incident had ended there. Chuck had never told Tammy about what had happened, fearing that she'd never let him out of the house again, but now, facing the machine in front of him—he wondered, was there some sort of military file on him, built around that picture the man had taken of him at the Area 51 overlook? Or did it even matter? His belief that someone might have been keeping tabs on him between Roswell and Area 51 meant that he would probably set off the polygraph. So he needed to be honest, whether that got him kicked out of the program or not.

"I'm not sure how to answer the question," he said. "There might be a file on me somewhere. But I bet it's mostly blacked out."

His joke fell flat as the officer continued staring at him. Then the officer exhaled and asked, "Mr. Zukowski, did you commit any crimes, like trespassing, at Roswell or Area 51?"

Chuck shook his head.

"Then let me reword the question. Outside of Roswell and the Area 51 incident, do you have any police files you know about that you haven't told the sheriff's department?"

"No, sir."

Chuck was pretty sure that it would be the strangest exchange ever recorded by the Colorado Springs Reserve Sheriff's Department Polygraph Test.

# CHAPTER 12

## COLORADO SPRINGS, COLORADO,
## JULY 4, 2002

The July 4 neighborhood barbecue was already in full swing by the time Chuck pulled his pitch-black Dodge Ram 1500 pickup truck into the driveway of his two-story home, on their tree-lined cul-de-sac in a bedroom suburb of Colorado Springs. Although the grill itself was two houses over in the front yard of the local high school principal, a fifty-something, hippyish former college biology professor, the crowd spilled down most of the block. Chuck counted at least a dozen of his neighbors in the manicured glade of grass in front of his own front stoop, with Tammy somewhere near the center of the group, handing out firework-themed cookies from an overloaded plastic tray. The kids were nowhere to be seen, which made sense; the oral surgeon who lived across the street had a swimming pool, and it was at least ninety degrees outside.

The parade detail had been brutal. Chuck had stood in the sun by a barricade for three hours until another reserve deputy showed up to take his place. There'd been a few snatched purses, a few locked cars, and at one point, Chuck had administered first aid to an elderly woman suffering from heatstroke, but the paramedics from the nearby Red Cross tent had relieved him before he'd had to do anything beyond applying cold compresses to the woman's head. He was tired and hungry, but also satisfied; the mere act of being in public in full uniform, helping people and eliciting the nods and smiles that came with a sheriff's badge in a relatively small mountain town, made him forget that he was a volunteer. He didn't need to be paid to love being a cop, any more than he expected to ever get rich off hunting UFOs.

He killed the engine of the truck and stepped out onto his driveway. He was still in uniform, but he'd checked his gun and equipment belt in his locker back at the department. He had plenty of guns locked up in various cabinets all over his house. His badge, volunteer though it was, kept anyone who knew about it from questioning his weapon collection. And the pickup—pitch-black, with dark windows—was fairly common in this part of the country.

Still, as he approached the crowd of neighbors milling around his lawn, he sensed the slightest bit of apprehension behind some of the smiles and waves.

Chuck had done what he could to keep his interest in UFOs separate from his work at the department—other than the episode with the polygraph, he'd never talked about his investigations while on official business. Nor had he ever worn his uniform for anything other than legitimate police work. But in his personal life, he'd happily broadcast his interests to anyone who would listen. His big personality had him holding court at numerous neighborhood functions, dinner parties, and holiday barbecues—which was actually part of his investigative strategy. The more he talked about UFOs and advanced himself as an expert in the field, the more people brought him stories of their own. In his mind, his method wasn't that different from police work; when cops were looking for information on a suspect, they'd put the man's picture in the paper. The louder the megaphones, the more frequent the informants.

Despite Chuck's best efforts, his openness to his neighbors about his interests eventually did trickle into his professional life, both at the microchip company and at the police department.

When his colleagues learned of his hobby, the nicknames became inevitable. "UFO Nut" was Chuck's favorite, which he eagerly co-opted, and even put on his license plate. It made him seem harmless, a sort of intentional form of camouflage. But his colleagues at the sheriff's department called him "the Mulder of El Paso," after the lead character in the popular science-fiction show *The X-Files*.

The nickname had quickly circulated through the entire county police department. At first, Chuck had resisted the title; he didn't like being compared to a character who pretty much believed in everything. But then a funny thing began to happen. Because of the nickname, every time something unusual occurred in or near El Paso, from reports of strange lights in the sky, to sightings of unidentifiable animals in the nearby pine forests, to unexplained events in the mountains or on the many Indian reservations in the area, he'd get a call.

Sometimes it was as simple as an officer waiting until he had gotten Chuck alone, then leaning in to tell him that, yeah, he'd seen a UFO out on night patrol. Other times, it was something more significant. On one occasion, Chuck had been working an accident scene downtown when two city cops who were also SWAT members had pulled him aside:

"You're that guy, right? The UFO expert?"

And before Chuck had been able to answer, they'd launched into a story about an incident from one week earlier, when they had been tasked with clearing out an abandoned school after a parking lot shooting. The SWAT team had been working with a dog handler and a trained scent dog, a German shepherd with years of on-duty experience. They had been walking the dog through a classroom when suddenly the dog had stopped dead, turning and barking furiously. For whatever reason, the dog wouldn't let them pass. When they'd finally calmed the animal and gotten him outside, they'd heard from other officers that witnesses had spotted three triangular craft flying in formation high above the school.

The SWAT officers hadn't reported the incident for fear of what the department might think. But they'd wanted to tell someone—and Chuck, UFO Nut, the Mulder of El Paso, was the perfect sympathetic ear.

Still, Chuck knew that for every colleague who accepted his outside interests, there were probably three who just thought he was crazy. At the barbecue, he reached Tammy and her tray of pastries after shaking hands with neighbors welcoming him to his own yard. As he approached, a few of the couples made their way out of the group. The handful that remained mostly had kids the same age as Chuck and Tammy's or were newer to the neighborhood.

Tammy no doubt noticed the shift in the immediate population, as well, but her face didn't show it. If anything, her concern was for Chuck and the likelihood that he was going to say something off-the-wall or inappropriate.

For the first ten minutes, her concern was unwarranted; the conversation trended to topics ranging from Chuck's duties as a deputy sheriff to the recent rise in real estate values. And then one of the newer neighbors on the block happened to mention that his family was Mormon. Chuck had immediately launched into a discussion about something he'd read: that Mormons always kept supplies of food and water somewhere in their homes in case of natural disasters, called the Year's Supply. Chuck had been fascinated by the notion of a church edict to be prepared and found it oddly similar to the Native American Anasazi's habit of building their homes high along cliff walls, which hadn't done them very much good, in the end.

"You don't think it's good practice to store supplies?" the neighbor asked. "In case of emergency?"

"The way I see it," Chuck said, "I don't need to store food and water. I've got a lot of guns. In an emergency, all I need is a map to all the nearby Mormons."

The pause before the Mormon neighbor laughed was long enough for Tammy to give Chuck a dozen inaudible signals that he'd be spending the rest of the barbecue safely upstairs in his office, surrounded by his file cabinets and his UFOs.

. . .

The office window was closed, since the central air-conditioning was on, and the shades were drawn, but Chuck left the door open a crack so he could still smell the hot dogs from the grill down below. Here, in his office, he was in his own world, surrounded by the hundreds of souvenirs from his years of family road trips, the assorted paraphernalia that he'd collected over more than a decade of amateur UFO hunting, and his stuffed file cabinets, bookshelves, and desk. His boys called it his Batcave; but to Chuck, it was less lair, more working laboratory.

Recently, he'd put up a large whiteboard along one wall, directly above his computer. The whiteboard was one of the cheapest pieces of equipment he'd purchased since they'd moved to Colorado, but in many ways it had become the centerpiece of his study, the focus of whatever area of interest he was investigating at any particular moment. For many months, the whiteboard had been filled with sketches of mutilated animals. As the Mulder of El Paso, he'd been handed so many mutilation cases, he'd needed to add two levels to his tower of file cabinets.

Since then, he'd shifted from animal mutilations back to UFOs, covering the whiteboard with case files from dozens of recent sightings, using different-colored pens to categorize the different types of craft, and the way they had appeared to move across the sky.

And in recent days, he'd decided to take a step back; start again, from a more holistic perspective.

He wasn't quite sure what had prompted him to retrieve a huge map of the United States from one of his storage shelves, but for whatever reason, he'd carefully attached the map across the whiteboard. The map had been so big, he'd needed to tear down a large poster of Mickey Mouse wearing a space suit that he'd bought during a family trip to Disney—

after a slight detour to a nearby suburb where Chuck had interviewed a woman who had claimed to have been abducted by aliens—to make room. Then he'd carefully begun charting his UFO and animal mutilation reports on the map, using colored pins to denote their precise geographical locations.

He was taking the exercise slowly, methodically. In two days, he'd added only a half dozen reports to the map. He wasn't looking for anything in particular; he just wanted to create something visible to study. Getting through all the case files in his cabinets would take months, perhaps years, but he wasn't in any hurry. His only plan was to give himself a bit of inspiration, as he planned out his road trips. He figured that seeing the pins spread out across the map would give him some sense of how pervasive these anomalies truly were.

Standing there, breathing in the scent of grilling hot dogs, listening to the dull hum of the party outside, shifting over the six colored pins that he'd already put up—one red pin over the school where the SWAT members had reported the triangular craft, a yellow pin above a mutilation in San Luis Valley, on and on—he was concentrating so fully that he didn't hear the door behind him pushing open or the footsteps against the floor. He didn't notice anyone else in the room with him, until a small shadow crept across the sleeping screen of his computer.

He turned to see his daughter, Ashley, right next to him, her arms crossed in copycat fashion to his own, staring up with him at the map.

"What happened to Mickey?"

Maybe she was too young to know what the map might mean or maybe she didn't care that her father was walking that line between hobby and obsession, curiosity and crazy.

Or maybe to a kid who already believed in Mickey Mouse, UFOs were a pretty easy sell.

# CHAPTER 13

## RUSH, COLORADO,
## AUGUST 12, 2010

At Glenda's ranch house, it took three of them to finally corner her dog in the first-floor kitchen. Glenda, Chuck, and a ranch hand trapped him between an aging GE icebox and a stained wooden cutlery cabinet. Glenda held his trembling muzzle, talking in soothing tones into his ear, while one of her ranch hands got hold of his hindquarters, trying to stay out of the way of his rapidly kicking rear paws. Chuck was down on his knees next to the poor animal, who was piercing their ears with his high-pitched whines.

The dog's terrified behavior was frightening enough, but the EMF reader was singing at levels Chuck hadn't seen in a long time. As he ran the receiver over the strange lacerations on the animal's left front leg, the Trifield spiked over one hundred microteslas. *Twice the magnetic field of the Earth.* Chuck had run the EMF meter over dogs before, never recording anything above six microteslas.

"That's not normal, is it?" Glenda said.

Chuck switched hands, retrieving a metal-detecting wand from his equipment pack. He moved closer to the lacerations, careful not to cause the animal any pain. The cuts didn't appear to be bleeding or oozing pus.

They didn't look like burns, nor did they seem to have been cauterized, but they were certainly deeper than scrapes, and it was unlikely the animal could have inflicted them on himself.

The metal detector didn't measure any type of metallic inserts. Gently probing the wounds with his gloved fingers, Chuck couldn't feel any internal abnormalities. No scar tissue, nothing that seemed artificial.

"Damnedest thing," Glenda said, struggling to hold on to the animal's muzzle. "Normally he's outside every minute he can be, roaming the grounds. Now he sits in here, whining and crying. I tried forcing him out this morning, he just sat right on the porch, scratching at the door to get back in."

There was no doubt in Chuck's mind that the dog and the surviving horse, who had been with the two mutilated animals when they'd died, had witnessed something traumatic.

"The night it happened, he was howling bloody murder. I had to go out and quiet him down three times. Wasn't until I found the bodies the next morning that I realized he'd had good reason to howl. The two of them, lying there like that, so frozen and rigid, they looked like plastic toys. The dog just ran to the house, but King, the yearling, got in front of me, tried to stop me from getting near the bodies. Don't know if she was trying to protect them—or me."

Chuck gave the ranch hand the signal to free the poor canine. Glenda whispered one more time into Cody's ear, and then he was gone, streaking deeper into the interior of the house.

"I'd like to take a closer look at King," said Chuck.

Chuck had expected this investigation would be a quick mission, since he was there so many days after the event and the police had already come and gone. He'd assumed he'd get a few readings, take some pictures and notes, and add the case to his growing files. But the surviving dog and King made this case unique.

As they exited the house and walked back toward the corral, Glenda picked up on the conversation they had started by the two corpses.

"How can this be going on for so long, in so many places, without the government getting involved? I mean, unless the government *is* involved."

Chuck understood her meaning. Plenty of people who'd researched the phenomenon had come to the conclusion that many, if not all, of the mutilations had something to do with secret military projects. It was not uncommon for ranchers and other witnesses to come forward after a police report, telling stories of seeing black, unmarked helicopters near mutilation sites, as well as other flying craft, of various shapes and sizes, zigzagging over the spots where bodies had been found. One of the most famous modern-era cattle mutilation sites, a ranch owned by the Gomez family located near the peak of the Archuleta Mesa, thirteen miles from Dulce, New Mexico, had lost upward of fifty head of cattle to mutilations in incidents spanning the years between 1975 and 1983. An investigation headed by a local police officer, Gabe Valdez, had turned up numerous links to unknown military assets, including evidence of some sort of aircraft landing in the vicinity, traces of radiation at the mutilation site, unknown nerve agents and sedatives found in the carcasses' tissue, and reports of unknown craft as well as unmarked black helicopters in the area.

At Rush, Glenda herself had heard a helicopterlike sound around the time the dog was howling outside her house, but nobody else had reported choppers in the vicinity.

For Chuck, black helicopters had become such a cultural meme connected with all types of paranormal phenomena that he didn't like heading down that route without some sort of evidence beyond a "whooshing" sound the night of an incident. But that didn't mean the government hadn't ever involved itself in investigations of animal mutilations: quite the opposite.

"The government is well aware of these mutilations," Chuck said. "In the seventies, there were so many cases—many of them here, in Colorado—that it was reaching the front pages of newspapers across the country. At first, the FBI tried to avoid digging into the phenomenon, claiming that it didn't indicate any ongoing threat to the nation. It took a United States senator from Colorado to force them to acknowledge that something dangerous was going on."

Senator Floyd Haskell sent a letter to the head of the FBI office in Denver, one of the first official documents to recognize that cattle mutilations were more than just some symptom of mass hysteria. The FBI might not have felt threatened by thousands of mutilated animals left in fields, in the middle of the night, missing eyes and ears and sexual organs, but Coloradans—and their senator—felt differently (see letter on page 88).

"So the FBI opened an investigation?" Glenda asked after Chuck told her about Senator Haskell's letter. As she and Chuck reached the corral, she opened the gate and led Chuck inside.

"No, even that wasn't enough. But the newspapers picked up the senator's letter. First the *Denver Post*, a few days later, on September 3, 1975. The *Post*, alarmed that the FBI wasn't getting involved, suggested that the senator take the matter to Congress. The *Post* reported that the situation had gotten so bad that a 'gun-happy frame of mind' had developed in the affected areas, so bad that the Bureau of Land Management had stopped sending helicopters to inventory land in six counties, because they were afraid their copters would get shot down."

Glenda pointed out King near the back of the corral, nervously pawing at the ground, just as he'd been doing when Chuck had first arrived at the ranch. Chuck understood the "gun-happy frame of mind" that had floated across the area back in the seventies. Regular poachers were threatening enough; something that came after your cattle in the middle of the night, leaving the bodies mutilated in such a vicious manner— Chuck wouldn't have wanted to fly a helicopter over a ranch that had just lost an animal like that.

# United States Senate
WASHINGTON, D.C. 20510

August 29, 1975

Theodore P. Rosack
Special Agent In Charge
Denver Federal Building
1961 Stout Street
Denver, Colorado 80202

Dear Mr. Rosack:

For several months my office has been receiving reports of cattle mutilations throughout Colorado and other western states. At least 130 cases in Colorado alone have been reported to local officials and the Colorado Bureau of Investigation (CBI); the CBI has verified that the incidents have occured for the last two years in nine states.

The ranchers and rural residents of Colorado are concerned and frightened by these incidents. The bizarre mutilations are frightening in themselves: in virtually all the cases, the left ear, left eye, rectum and sex organ of each animal has been cut away and the blood drained from the carcass, but with no traces of blood left on the ground and no footprints.

In Colorado's Morgan County area, there has also been reports that a helicopter was used by those who mutilated the carcasses of the cattle, and several persons have reported being chased by a similar helicopter.

Because I am gravely concerned by this situation, I am asking that the Federal Bureau of Investigation enter the case. Although the CBI has been investigating the incidents, and local officials also have been involved, the lack of a central unified direction has frustrated the investigation. It seems to have progressed little, except for the recognition at long last that the incidents must be taken seriously.

Now it appears that ranchers are arming themselves to protect their livestock, as well as their families and themselves, because they are frustrated by the unsuccessful investigation. Clearly something must be done before someone gets hurt.

63-0-36721

ENCLOSURE

Page 2

The fact that allegations have been made of the loss of livestock in 21 states under similar circumstances strongly suggests the very real possibility that the crossing of state lines is involved and, this alone, I feel, should justify the participation of the FBI in this case.

I urge you to begin your investigation as soon as possible, and to contact my office to discuss in more detail the incidents I have described. We stand ready to give you all possible assistance.

Sincerely,

Floyd K. Haskell
United States Senator

FKH:emw

---

"Articles appeared all over the place, day after day. Most were similar to the *Post* article, demanding that someone official investigate the matter. Other media tried to conduct their own investigations. One of the most comprehensive was by a magazine, *Oui*, a porn magazine started in France that had migrated to the U.S. under Hugh Hefner as an addendum to *Playboy*. In September 1976, the writer Ed Sanders advanced two theories. One was that the military was testing biological weapons on unsuspecting cattle and removing their organs to read for results of biological agents, for future use in warfare."

They had been walking toward King and now were only a few feet from the yearling. Glenda had both hands out, calming the horse before they moved any closer. Chuck wasn't sure if he was giving her more information than she'd expected or wanted. Sometimes, when he got started on a topic, he just couldn't stop.

"The second theory was even more bizarre. According to the author's research, a former Leavenworth inmate had alleged to police that a group of Satan-worshipping bikers had developed a widespread cattle mutilation fetish. The group had supposedly operated across multiple states, and had devised a sophisticated system: They used the tranquilizing drug PCP to calm the cattle, switched to amyl nitrite to make the animals' hearts beat rapidly, then withdrew all of the blood using large veterinary syringes."

"You're kidding," Glenda said. She had both hands on King, and the horse had finally stopped pawing.

"It gets stranger. Supposedly, the satanic bikers didn't leave any footprints at the crime scenes because they placed pieces of cardboard on the ground around the animals to walk on, which they later removed. If there was snow, they used fire and blowtorches to get rid of their footprints. They wanted it to look like UFOs were mutilating the cattle, to keep anyone from figuring them out."

It sounded ludicrous, but according to the article, the allegations had led to a police investigation involving officers from multiple states. Even so, it wasn't a porno magazine, satanic bikers, or the *Denver Post* that finally led the FBI to get involved.

"It took another senator—this time from New Mexico—writing a letter to the attorney general of the United States to finally get the federal government interested."

It had been the Gomez family, whose ranch near Dulce had lost over fifty head of cattle, estimated in value at over a hundred thousand dollars, who had contacted Senator Harrison Schmitt and first gotten him involved in the mutilation phenomenon. The mutilations themselves were unnerving; the thought that some surreptitious agency within the military might be involved seemed positively sinister.

As the *Oui* article illustrated: *And then there were the helicopters. Helicopters without filed flight plans were sighted quite often in the afflicted counties, sometimes hovering above cattle pens. Were the helicopters evi-*

*dence that some branch of the military was involved in the mutilations themselves, or part of a secret investigation after the fact?*

"The senator had immediately understood the seriousness of the situation—whether what was happening near Dulce was related somehow to some secretive military project or was the work of something even more bizarre, it needed to be investigated. The senator's letter, in turn, had finally gotten the import of the situation across to someone with the power to start an investigation. The attorney general's response was unequivocal: 'I must say that the materials sent me indicate the existence of one of the strangest phenomena in my memory.' Three years later, on April 20, 1979, Schmitt hosted a major conference dedicated to animal mutilations, in Albuquerque, New Mexico, which included more than 180 attendees: officers from various law enforcement agencies, media representatives, and experts both scientific and civilian. According to the FBI memorandum from the conference, theories were discussed that included 'satanic cults, predators, pranksters, extraterrestrials, and unknown government agencies.'"

Chuck said, "Finally, by 1980, a formal investigation was funded and announced."

Chuck stepped past Glenda with his equipment, and began his survey of the skittish yearling, starting at the strange circular mark that had been left on the animal's muzzle.

The spot felt smooth, flush with the skin. Chuck couldn't feel anything obvious underneath, and King didn't seem to mind Chuck's touching the area with his fingers. Chuck didn't find any EMF spiking at all—certainly nothing like what he'd found on the dog—and had no radiological or metallic readings.

He found odd, oval marks on the inside of the horse's front legs, as well as a three-quarter-inch circular discoloration above King's left shoulder blade, next to a V-shaped pair of lacerations. He got no readings from these areas, either.

"Nineteen eighty," Glenda said. "That's thirty years ago."

Chuck stepped back from the yearling. Just looking at the animal's eyes, the way they darted back and forth, he knew the poor creature would never be the same. From the expression on Glenda's pale face, he guessed that she, too, would be permanently changed by whatever had happened on her ranch.

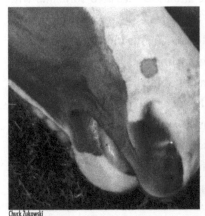 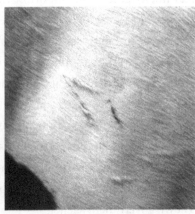

Chuck Zukowski

He wished that he could tell her something that would somehow make this better. He wished he could help her understand what had happened. Hell, he was determined, someday, to have answers.

But for the moment, like the FBI, he had nothing but theories.

"Thirty years," he said. "God only knows how many agents, how much money, how many letters from senators and FBI memos. And we're still right where we started."

Turning away from the corral, he could taste the rancid scent of the two dead horses in the breeze.

# CHAPTER 14

## RIVERSIDE NATIONAL CEMETERY,
## RIVERSIDE, CALIFORNIA,
## OCTOBER 8, 2002

They came out of the low clouds in perfect formation, moving fast, cutting an elliptical arc through the breezeless sky, no more than a thousand feet above the ground. Four of them, flying so close together it seemed as if the wings were almost touching. From below, the craft looked like airborne metal crosses, etched with old numbers and insignia, sunlight flashing off the visible rivets and the polished glass curves of their pilot canopies.

Without warning, the lead craft cut hard left, leaving the formation, while the other three vessels continued across the sky. With a tilt of the wings left, then right, the first craft suddenly dived straight for the ground. For a brief moment, Chuck actually held his breath, thinking that maybe something had gone wrong, that the thing was going to crash right down into the cemetery—but then, at the very last moment, the pilot pulled up on the throttle, heading straight back up, higher and higher, until he was lost again in the clouds.

"That was incredible," Chuck said, watching the other three planes growing smaller as they sped past the cemetery. "Dad would have loved it. A flyover of vintage military planes. Hell of a coincidence."

Chuck's brother Ron, in his Class A uniform from the Coast Guard Reserve, had already stepped out of earshot, comforting their other brother, Andy, in his own Homeland Security dress costume, by the entrance to the funeral home where they'd just brought their father's casket for the ceremony—but the retired navy chaplain who was going to perform the rites was still to Chuck's left, going through the notes Chuck had put together on his father's service record. The chaplain gave Chuck's shoulder a squeeze.

"It wasn't a coincidence, son."

As it turned out, once a month a squadron of vintage World War II planes flew over the Riverside National Cemetery in memory of a decorated soldier. When the navy chaplain had heard about Chuck's father's service—and seen the medals the man had accrued—he'd arranged the exercise. Not just a simple flyover; the lead plane had broken off from the rest to honor the lost soldier.

Chuck knew that if any soldier deserved such a display, it was his father. A member of the Sixty-eighth Tank Battalion in the Sixth Armor Division under Patton's Third Army, the older Zukowski had earned four service stars for duty for the landing at Normandy, the Battle of the Bulge, the liberation of Paris, and entering the Rhineland. Although his father had never spoken about Normandy or the Battle of the Bulge, Chuck knew that he'd served proudly, and that he'd developed many lifelong friendships through the military.

He'd been a good father, more straitlaced and rigid than Chuck was, but open-minded enough to accept Chuck for who he was. Many nights, he'd even listened to Chuck's stories about his UFO and animal mutilation investigations. He hadn't been a believer, but he'd never hung up the phone, no matter how long the calls had been.

Chuck would say a few words in his eulogy about his father's willingness to listen, though he'd promised himself not to bring up UFOs, at least not unless someone else brought them up first.

Chuck wasn't the only member of the Zukowski clan to focus seriously on UFOs and other such phenomena. Just that morning, when the family had first gathered for breakfast to talk about his father's life, Chuck learned that his sister, Debbie, had not only developed an interest in UFOs, she was now rising up the ranks of the Missouri chapter of MUFON. Chuck had initially been dismayed that she'd chosen to see past what he considered to be serious issues with the national UFO research network. But she'd told him that her own experiences with MUFON had been nothing but positive. She understood his concerns, but she was impressed by the people she was working with at MUFON, and also believed that being inside the network would give her access to information, cases, and research she could never find elsewhere.

In the end, Chuck was simply impressed that she'd dedicated herself to the cause, independently of his own quest for answers. As the navy chaplain went back to his notes, reading about Chuck's father's time under Patton, Chuck glanced toward his sister, who was standing by her husband, Wayne, near their rental car at the edge of the parking lot, a few yards from the gate leading into the cemetery. She and Wayne weren't alone; Chuck's octogenarian aunt Petra and her daughter Flora were leaning very close, telling a story that obviously had caught Debbie's interest.

Chuck's curiosity pulled him away from the chaplain, and he made short work of the distance, arriving just in time to hear Petra launch into a story he'd never heard before.

On Interstate 40 on the California-Arizona border, in 1952—five years after the events at Roswell—Petra had been traveling with her husband, Roy, and their three small kids toward their home in Morenci, Arizona, after visiting relatives in Long Beach, California. According to Petra, at around one in the morning her husband had decided to pull over by the side of the highway to get some sleep. The average speed on the interstate in the early fifties was below 60 mph, so it would generally take at least ten hours to get to their destination, with nowhere worth stopping along the way. Since there were no rest areas at the time, pulling off the highway for sleep was a fairly common strategy.

Petra hadn't been tired at the time, so she just relaxed in the front passenger seat while the rest of the family fell asleep. After an hour, she noticed something in the distance. A group of small people, as she described them, were walking toward the car from the direction of the desert.

As they got closer, she had realized they weren't people at all.

Terrified and unable to speak, she had covered her eyes with her hands—but eventually she forced herself to look. Petra's description was the same as those from dozens of similar stories he'd heard, from descriptions of the bodies supposedly found at Roswell to a report he'd taken outside Denver just weeks earlier. Petra had seen classic Grays—perhaps the most common alien type described at sightings. Short, hairless, with large, bulbous heads, no discernible features other than big black cat eyes, unremarkable orifices instead of noses and ears, and small mouths. Most were described as gray or dark gray, though some reports Chuck had taken had trended toward metallic shades, even blue.

As Petra paused, obviously shaken by her own retelling of the story, her daughter explained that she'd woken up in the backseat and sat up and watched her mom frantically looking around. Then her mom told her to lie back down. Flora herself had never seen anything, but she believed her mother's story.

Chuck's own mother had told him a few times that she'd been visited by extraterrestrials when she was a child. In fact, she was certain that her heart palpitations were the result of the frightening visits, which usually came at night, beginning when she was a toddler. Chuck had never delved too deeply into her stories, realizing that there was no way to find any sort of evidence or corroborating witnesses, but he'd always assumed that her stories had fed his own willingness to believe.

Aunt Petra's "close encounter" was no more verifiable than his mother's, but it was intriguing to hear, especially alongside Debbie. His own investigations had always felt like a little nuclear family business, but now he knew he had other connections. His sister could prove valuable in his own research. The sheriff's department gave him access to local reports and the observations of fellow officers, but Debbie was hooked into a national UFO network, well beyond his own association with the organization. An alliance with Debbie—and through her, MUFON—might lead him further than he could go on his own.

Chuck had always had a good relationship with his sister, and his wife, Tammy, wasn't going to go out into the field with him. Hell, a month earlier, he'd taken her out at night to a nearby pasture to try out new night-vision goggles he'd bought from a pawn shop. She'd gotten a few feet ahead of him, wearing the goggles, when suddenly she'd started screaming. Apparently, she'd nearly walked right into a cow, coming in face-first so that the animal's eyes had filled her entire field of vision. For a brief moment, she'd thought she was about to be the first case of a bovine abduction.

Debbie was different. She was an avid outdoorswoman, competent in the field, with experience in diving. She and her husband ran a fire and water restoration company, restoring structures and equipment after natural and man-made disasters. She didn't talk as much as Chuck did, but maybe more important, she knew how to listen.

After Petra finished her story, Debbie offered what comfort she could, telling her aunt that she'd heard many similar tales in Missouri, and had whole casebooks filled with drawings of the sort of Grays Petra had described. Chuck had one question for his aunt.

"When the aliens were coming toward the car, can you remember how they moved?"

Petra looked at him for a moment. Then she took a step back, gestured for her daughter to give her room. When she was ready, she performed a sort of shuffle step, leaning forward, dragging her legs awkwardly behind her body. As she moved, the bottoms of her feet never left the pavement.

Debbie looked at Chuck, but he didn't explain. He asked this question of every witness who had reported a close encounter. The question seemed innocuous, but he had a reason for his query.

In all the research Chuck had done on first-person alien encounters, the way the aliens had moved was always described in the exact same way: *Hunched forward, shuffle step, feet always touching the ground.*

On its own, it didn't mean anything. To a skeptic, it was just another detail from an overimaginative mind. A piece of information from one case file matching another. Coincidence.

Like vintage military planes flying in formation, over a good soldier's funeral.

# CHAPTER 15

## UFO WATCHTOWER,
## HOOPER, COLORADO,
## MAY 24, 2002

**37.7458° N, 105.8769° W**

It was a little after one-thirty in the morning when Debbie saw the first light.

She was standing on a packing crate, her body braced against the high chain-link fence that ran around the top of the viewing platform, one hand guiding the telescope in a slow leftward arc. She was shifting past Mars through the edge of the constellation Virgo when she froze in place, wildly gesturing to Chuck with her free fingers.

"Got it! Bright orange, moving at a forty-five-degree angle—hold on, there's another one! Wait, there's even more."

She started to count off as Chuck hastily unzipped himself from his sleeping bag, where he had been resting next to the metal stairwell that ran down to the dome-shaped gift shop—now closed—below. The sleeping bag's zipper caught at the last tine, and it took him a good ten seconds to rip himself free. Then he was next to her at the fence, one foot on the packing crate, fighting the urge to just elbow her off the telescope so he could take his turn. Even though they were both adults, married, living in different states with lives of their own, she was still his big sister—and it was his telescope. He laughed at his own instincts, as she finally stepped aside to give him his turn.

"Thirteen of them," she whispered. "Came right up over the mountains behind the sand dunes. Three of them cut off at that forty-five-degree angle and headed straight down. The rest are still going up."

Chuck had no trouble seeing the lights. They were at least three times as big as Mars, which was still flickering at the edge of his sight line. From that distance, there was no underlying structure to the lights—they were just balls of brightness, a mix of orange and yellow. He believed they were moving too fast to be anything astronomical. He would have to check his star charts back at the RV to make sure, but for the moment, he felt certain he and Debbie were seeing an anomaly. Whether it was a UFO or some earthly event that could be explained, he didn't know. Although Debbie's enthusiasm was contagious, he was practical enough to understand that there were other reasons for lights like those: unexpected reflections, some sort of weather-testing device, falling satellite debris. But either way, it was a damn good first outing together, especially considering they hadn't actually come to Hooper to look at the sky.

He pulled back from the telescope, watching as his sister furiously began writing in her MUFON notebook, describing what they were seeing in matter-of-fact terms. He didn't need to read the words to know that she was getting the details right; Debbie was even more fastidious than he was, and just as enthusiastic. In the two days they'd been working with each other, he'd come to realize that he was both more of a skeptic and also more the "big picture" thinker, always looking for something bigger than the details themselves, a connection to other events, a commonality. Debbie was there for the facts and the stories. That made them a pretty good fit; added to that, the fact that they were brother and sister had its own advantages.

Chuck was pretty sure Tammy would have balked at the idea of his setting off on a weeklong investigation with a like-minded UFOlogist—an attractive, athletic blonde, with cascading curly hair and a tan that rivaled his own—if Debbie weren't his sister. Once Tammy approved the excursion, Debbie had flown to Colorado Springs, and they'd immediately set about planning their excursion.

From the start, they'd intended this to be a frequent partnership; three times a year, Debbie would leave her husband and her day job at their fire restoration company, and she and Chuck would make memories. Memorial Day weekend, Fourth of July, Labor Day—these would become four- to five-day tournaments searching for UFOs or related phenomena.

This Memorial Day weekend, Debbie had hit the ground running; Chuck had picked her up at the airport with his jeep and they had headed right out onto the road. By the time they'd parked in front of the first motel, eight hours in, they'd already drafted much of their game plan. Still, they'd spent almost the entire night wide awake in their shared single room, maps and notebooks spread out all over the two twin beds. Another perk of being related; they had no problem combining their resources.

Debbie was still Chuck's tough, tomboy big sister, who didn't let him get away with anything, and he was still the daredevil, annoying pain in her ass, always wanting to take charge. They shared a quirky sense of humor; sometime past midnight on that first evening, driving along a pitch-black stretch of highway, Chuck had gotten the idea to put on his night-vision goggles and douse the jeep's headlights. Debbie had quickly grabbed her own night-vision gear, and they had taken turns driving in complete darkness for the next sixty miles.

Likewise, they'd developed a working shorthand that played on their strengths. Debbie would take the lead in any interview sessions involving female witnesses, and Chuck would handle the old-school military types who might freeze up in front of a tough, independent woman. They also came up with a plan, in case they felt the need to go anywhere that was off-limits or less than legal; they would just say they were boyfriend and girlfriend, looking for a place to park.

Over the first night and early morning of driving, they'd also had a chance to talk about the coincidence of their obsessions; Debbie figured it had to do with their upbringings—not just their shared love of the sky and the stars, but also the order of their birth. Debbie had been the second child of six, and the second girl; there was no doubt in her mind that when she was born, their father had wanted a boy to even out her older sister. In every picture Debbie had of herself as a little kid, she was wearing a ball cap and blue jeans. When Chuck, the first boy in the family, had come along five years later, he had taken her place as the "first son"; but instead of resenting him for displacing her, Debbie had connected with him, and as children they'd become inseparable. By the time she'd moved off to Missouri and he'd gotten deeper into his motorcycles, microchips, and, unbeknownst to her, UFOs, they'd developed the same sort of independent streak.

As Debbie continued making her notes, Chuck rechecked the video camera attached to the telescope. He could still clearly see the balls of light—still rising above the saddlelike section of desert between the mountains and the dunes—and he couldn't wait to transfer the video to a bigger screen, so they could really analyze what they were seeing.

He could tell from Debbie's excitement that she was already invested in the idea that this was a true UFO sighting. Chuck wasn't going to discount the visual evidence in front of him, but for the moment it was just circumstantial. Still, he knew they were not the first people to see these lights. Judy Mesoline, who owned the spaceship-shaped shop downstairs, had built the observation structure here because of the frequency of sightings that had been reported over the years. Even so, Chuck and Debbie had ended up spending the first Friday night of their trip looking at the sky from the Watchtower mostly by accident. They had actually come to Hooper because of a horse.

For their first joint investigation, they'd kicked around a bunch of different possible sites. After Debbie had heard about Chuck's new-found fascination with animal mutilations, she'd suggested they start their trip by looking into the grandfather of the phenomenon—what had become known in UFOlogy as the mutilation of "Snippy the Horse." Snippy—whose real name was Lady, until an inventive, if macabre, journalist had decided Snippy had a better ring to it—was a three-year-old Appaloosa. Her body had been discovered brutally mutilated on a ranch in the San Luis Valley, just outside Hooper, back in 1967. It was the first nationally reported mutilation, and because it occurred at the same time as a number of UFO reports in the area, it quickly captured the national imagination.

Chuck had photos, diagrams, even vet autopsy reports about Snippy's case in his office file cabinets. As with the many mutilations that would come after, Snippy had been found lying on one side, some of the hide cut away to expose the body cavity. The animal's heart and brain were missing, along with other organs, and the bones that were visible had been bleached a strange white color. A visiting pathologist had been called in, and had reported that the injuries to the horse had appeared to be surgical in nature; he'd also noted, with surprise, that there was no blood found in or around the carcass.

As with the thousands of mutilations since, there were no animal or human tracks anywhere near the horse's body, nor were there any signs of struggle. According to the rancher who owned the horse and various witnesses who were present when the animal was found, there was, however, a strange circular indentation in a nearby field—which the rancher attributed to a "flying saucer." Furthermore, according to some reports by interviewers who returned to the scene over the next few years, that section of the ranch remained barren; no grass would grow there.

Even though the event was more than thirty years old, Chuck had agreed that it was a good exercise for their skills as investigators; there might be people who had been around during the Snippy years living near Hooper, and since Chuck was getting more and more reports of mutilations through his work with the sheriff's department and because he now lived in Colorado, he felt it was important to have a firm knowledge of the history of the first record of the phenomenon.

From the moment they hit Hooper, they'd thrown themselves deep into Snippy lore, beginning with a visit to a local museum dedicated to the incident. They also ventured out into the local community, trying to talk to as many people as they could about the case.

At first, they ran into a fair amount of reluctance among the locals; two outsiders asking questions about a long-dead horse led to a lot of doors slammed in their faces. But eventually they tracked down some knowledgeable sources in a nearby grocery store—Miss Deb's Convenience Store. These weren't first-person witnesses, but people who had grown up listening to the story from people who were around at the time of the event. By the end of the day, Chuck had managed to fill most of a notebook with details.

They learned that Snippy's bones had been stored in a warehouse in Alamosa, and that there had been some sort of custody battle over them. They'd also learned about numerous other mutilations on ranches in the area since the sixties. They also talked to a handful of UFO enthusiasts who lived in the area, including two women who claimed to be abductees; there wasn't any clear relationship between the women's stories and Snippy, but Chuck added their stories to the notebook anyway.

At that point, he and his sister were satisfied that they'd uncovered as much information as they were going to get, thirty years on from the mutilation. They'd been about to head back to the jeep when someone had suggested that they interview one more person, Judy Mesoline, a longtime Hooper resident and former rancher who was knowledgeable about Snippy the Horse and also had her own stories about UFO sightings in the area. She'd seen so many, in fact, that she had been inspired to open the gift shop and UFO Watchtower.

When they saw the domed construction and the metal-framed observation deck, Chuck and Debbie had immediately changed their plans for the evening. At worst, they would spend one night gazing at the stars through a telescope, like back when they were kids, fighting over who could spot Mars first. To them, even without moving lights in the sky, the view from the deck was as stunning at night as it was during the day.

Neither of them had expected to actually see anything—let alone capture it on video.

Chuck Zukowski

As the seconds passed, Chuck went back and forth between the recorder and the telescope's eyepiece, watching in silence until the last of the red-orange balls of light finally disappeared into the starlit sky.

"I think that's it," he said. Debbie finally looked up from her notebook.

"This is going to make one hell of a report," she said. "And here I thought I was just going to head back to Missouri with a stuffed Snippy from the gift shop downstairs. Who would have guessed I'd end up the subject of our own field investigation."

Chuck didn't respond right away. She was only half kidding, because she didn't just share his interests, she was also a card-carrying field agent for MUFON.

To be technically accurate, at the moment Chuck was, too. Before Debbie had headed to Colorado Springs to join him for the weekend, she had somehow persuaded him to reactivate his own membership in the national UFO network. He hadn't changed his position on the agency—he still had his suspicions—but he'd been willing to re-engage to keep Debbie happy. He knew her own association with MUFON went much deeper.

Like Chuck, Debbie had begun going to MUFON conferences and meetings after reading about the organization in an ad in a magazine. But unlike Chuck, she'd immediately liked being part of a national organization dedicated to uncovering UFOs and had set out to become an official field investigator. She'd gone through the training process, memorized the study manual, and headed out with other investigators on trial cases, learning how to conduct a case from the ground up. Chuck knew from his own MUFON manuals and from what Debbie had told him that MUFON evidentiary techniques mirrored police investigative strategies; in fact, the MUFON Field Investigator's Manual had many similarities to the manuals Chuck had studied in the Sheriff's Citizens' Academy, aside from a curiously stated "code of ethics":

### SECTION II, THE FIELD INVESTIGATOR'S CODE OF ETHICS
*by Ron Westrum, Ph.D.*
*2.1 OBJECTIVES OF THE CODE OF ETHICS*

> *The objectives of the Code of Ethics are: to promote free and dispassionate investigation of UFO sightings with due regard to the rights of the percipients; to promote an understanding of the aims of MUFON by percipients and the community in general; and, to protect MUFON and its representatives from public censure and legal problems.*

The tenets that followed included scientific detachment and honesty, advising investigators to always conduct themselves as if they were scientific researchers, maintaining objectivity in every case and aiming to find the truth of each incident. Investigators were also advised to inform anyone involved in the incident that they were affiliated with MUFON and how they would record any information they were told or uncovered, and what they would do with that information. They were urged to be sincere in their interest and objectives and not to seek to sensationalize any findings or exaggerate MUFON's role compared with other investigators'.

It also said:

> *The investigator should not encourage delusional thinking, nor insist upon a narrow and dogmatic interpretation of the facts. False hope of fame or profit should not be used to get witnesses to talk.*

And it advised investigators to share their own assessments of the incident with those who had reported and experienced it.

Chuck was also impressed by the equipment, also delineated in the MUFON Field Manual, much of which Debbie had with her in her backpack and in the metal-lined trunk that was now tucked into the back of Chuck's jeep. The mandated equipment list paralleled what he himself had collected through police channels and from pawn shops over the years. Fingerprinting kits, night vision, tape for cordoning, various cameras, specimen vials and bags—just a small sample of what the field manual suggested she bring with her on an official excursion.

## SECTION IV, THE FIELD INVESTIGATOR'S KIT
*by Raymond E. Fowler*

### 4.1 NECESSARY EQUIPMENT

*Although the Investigator will generally not always employ all of the items in this list during any given investigation, such items, nevertheless, should be readily accessible to him when the need arises. Thus, it would be advantageous to store these items in a special box, suitcase or briefcase.*

- *MUFON Identification Card*
- *Camera and film*
- *MUFON Questionnaire Forms*
- *Sample Containers (plastic bags)*
- *Investigator's Manual*
- *Tape measure, Ruler*
- *Compass (good quality)*
- *Flashlight (extra batteries)*
- *Clipboard or 3-ring notebook*
- *Farmers Almanac*
- *Area maps*
- *Magnifying Glass*
- *Paper*

- *String*
- *Pencils, pen*
- *Knife*
- *Star finder*
- *Tweezers*

The manual continued with two more lists of "desirable" equipment that could be helpful to the investigator, which included a tape recorder, shovel and small trowel, boots, binoculars, disposable gloves, chalk lines, and paraffin or plaster of Paris.

Optional equipment, which would be helpful only to investigators with a science background, included a Geiger counter, a scintillation spectrometer, a magnetometer UFO radiometer, topographical and aerial maps, and a police radiomonitor, if that were legal to possess.

Chuck was likewise impressed by the professional-looking case file system employed by the organization, from how MUFON classified its various investigations, to how they handled witness information.

Debbie had gone through the various categories of UFO incidents with him before they'd set out on their trip: beginning with a C1 (a close encounter involving a craft five hundred feet away or closer); then to a C2 (an encounter with some sort of evidence left behind, such as an EMF reading); to a C3 (an encounter that included witness reports of alien beings); to a C4 (reports of a witness being taken aboard a craft and interacting with said aliens); to, finally, a C5 (an encounter that ended with permanent damage or even death).

Lights through a telescope, even videotaped, might barely be a C1, but Debbie was already thinking about the report she'd like to submit when she got home to Missouri. Chuck was technically a MUFON colleague, but he didn't like the direction Debbie's thoughts were heading. He didn't see this four-day trip as a MUFON investigation; he'd already told Debbie as much before they'd set off on the road. Now that they'd possibly seen something, he didn't want her excitement to change what this trip was about.

"Let's just leave MUFON out of this for now," Chuck said. "We don't even know what it is we've just seen. We need to check our star charts, then put those lights on a bigger screen."

Debbie looked at him, and for a moment he thought she was going to push back. Twenty years earlier, when they were still teenagers, she might have done more than push back, she might have shoved him off the observation deck. But instead, she simply shrugged.

"Fair enough, we can wait and see what we've got."

Like Chuck, she had talked to many witnesses of similar sightings who had been fooled by airplanes, helicopters, weather anomalies, and tricks of light.

"If it's something worth a deeper look, we can always come back. Hell, by next Memorial Day, they'll probably have built a rotating hotel, with a neon Snippy the Horse on top."

# CHAPTER 16

## ZAPATA FALLS, COLORADO,
## JULY 4, 2002

It happened so fast, Chuck didn't have time to react. One minute the jeep was bouncing along the narrow trail, tires fighting against the jagged terrain, axles jerking upward over mogul-sized stones and moss-covered tree trunks; then without warning, the entire car seemed to be in the air, vaulted upward by a fallen branch as thick as a diesel smokestack. There was a moment of pure weightlessness—then the jeep came down hard, the front left tire exploding, pieces of shredded rubber pelting up toward the vehicle's windshield.

Chuck slammed on the brakes, stopping the wounded jeep dead in the middle of the path. For a brief moment, there was silence—then the sound of his daughter, Ashley, laughing joyfully from the backseat.

"Wow, that was awesome. Do it again!"

Chuck looked back at her, then at Debbie in the passenger seat next to him. His sister was already sticking her head out the side window, surveying the damage. From Chuck's vantage, he was pretty sure it was just the tire; he must have hit a sharp piece of shale when they'd come down after going over the fallen tree limb. He could have the tire changed in ten minutes, but looking ahead, at the winding path jerking and jagging up through the thick forest in front of them, he was pretty sure they'd gone as far as they were going to go. Though the park ranger's office near the sand dunes at the bottom of the trail had assured him that the trail was drivable, somewhere in the last mile the terrain had gotten noticeably worse. If Chuck had to guess, he'd say they were approaching a Class 9 traverse, bad enough if he'd been alone in the jeep, but even worse when he also had to worry about the safety of his daughter and sister.

He reached into the glove compartment and retrieved the map he'd downloaded off the Internet the day before. A quick glance confirmed that they still had four more miles to the top, and the terrain was only going to get worse as they neared Blanca Peak and the small lake nearby that was their original destination. Ashley was obviously enjoying the ride, but Chuck wasn't going to risk another tire, or worse—flipping the jeep over—with her in the backseat.

He didn't regret bringing his daughter along; like Debbie, she was his partner in crime, and she was especially pleased to be spending this special time with her dad and aunt. Tammy hadn't been able to refuse her the opportunity, but she'd made Chuck promise that it would be a "soft" investigation. Four-by-fouring up a Class 9 trail wasn't soft, no matter what the destination.

"I don't think we're going to make the lake," he said, handing the map to Debbie. "After I change the tire, we can turn back and park by the falls. It's still a pretty good view over the valley. If the lights come back, we'll be able to see them clearly from there."

Debbie didn't respond as he pushed his way out of the jeep and started for the trunk where he kept the jack and spare. Ashley was making faces at him through the rear window. He was sure Debbie was disappointed. From the research they'd conducted since seeing the lights from the UFO tower over Memorial Day, six weeks earlier, the small lake where they'd been headed, right snug against Blanca Peak, was supposedly ground zero for sightings. Through MUFON files, Debbie had even read that some investigators had begun to suspect there was some sort of underwater base where the lights were coming from, based on their trajectory—as wild as that sounded—and they had been hoping to spend the night camped out in the vicinity—though not too close—high-def video recorder at the ready.

But Zapata Falls would have to do. Though the thirty-foot waterfall cut through a secluded canyon near the base of the Sangre de Cristo Mountains, the parking area was at a high-enough elevation to provide a good view of the entire valley, including the dunes over which he and Debbie had seen the lights on their previous trip.

As Chuck went to work on the tire, he listened to his sister and daughter chatting away about UFOs, alien bases, and the worthlessness of brothers—especially brothers who apparently had much better things to do with their holidays than spend them out in the wilderness, looking for aliens. Ashley was excited about the prospect of seeing something out there in the sky. She had watched the video he and Debbie had taken over Memorial Day a dozen times already in the RV, which was parked down by the park ranger's station. Although the video was inconclusive—no matter how much Chuck had tried to enhance the image—they wanted to try to learn more about where the lights had been heading. He and Debbie hadn't been able to wait for the following Memorial Day, and he'd negotiated a Fourth of July excursion with Tammy. It was going to cost him a new dining room table, but with the high-def camera he'd found at a garage sale in Denver, he hoped this time he was going to come away from the area around Hooper with something that would impress even Tammy.

Twenty minutes later, they were back on the trail but moving in the other direction, retracing their way to the base of the falls. The ride was equally bumpy on the way down—the jeep catching air every few feet, while Chuck did his best to avoid any rocks sharp enough to wound the spare tire or do any damage to the axles—but he found the motion strangely soothing. Ashley felt the same, because, by the time they'd parked just outside the lot, front wheels feet from the edge of a rough slope leading down into the valley, she was horizontal on the backseat, fast asleep.

Chuck and Debbie worked quietly, using hand signals instead of words so as not to wake her as they set up their equipment for the night. Chuck propped the night-vision camera with the HD recorder on top of his tripod, right outside his jeep door. They intended to stay inside the vehicle all night, the engine running, the heat cranked up. The park ranger had warned them that both mountain lions and bears were in the area—something else he would avoid telling Tammy about when he got home—and he figured he could see plenty from behind the safety of the front windshield.

Once everything was ready to go, Chuck settled back behind the steering wheel, letting his head touch the vinyl of the seat behind him. The view in front of him was staggering, even at night. The stars and the Moon lit up half the valley, spread out like an open bowl in front of him, all the way to the wavelike dunes cresting along the horizon. It was almost as good a vantage point as the observation tower. Nature was going to give Judy Mesoline a hell of a run for that almighty tourist traffic. Combined with the soft rumble from the nearby falls, the spot seemed close to perfect. Chuck wasn't sure, exactly, when he dozed off, but when Debbie grabbed at his shoulder at 1:00 a.m., she needed both hands to shake him awake.

Her eyes were wide, and he followed her gaze out the front windshield.

*Christ.*

One. Two. Three. The lights just kept coming, rising right up above the dunes, shooting at incredible speeds right up over the valley until the siblings lost count. These lights weren't coming from the same location as the lights he and Debbie had seen over Memorial Day weekend, but they were just as bright, orange and red. There seemed to be twice as many as at the watchtower, maybe twenty-four, twenty-five balls of light following one another in a brightly glowing trail. And they were moving faster than those few in the last sighting, more erratically, almost bumping into one another as they rose higher and higher.

*Mountain lions and bears be damned.* Chuck leaped out the door of the jeep and grabbed the camera, swinging it in the direction of the lights. He made sure the thing was still recording, then did his best to focus on the trail, following the balls of light from the ground upward. He wasn't keeping track of the time, but it couldn't have been more than a minute, when just as suddenly as they had come, the lights vanished, leaving nothing but a tiny red-orange glare in Chuck's vision when he blinked his eyes.

"I can't believe it," Debbie whispered. Then she glanced back at Ashley, who was still fast asleep in the back of the jeep. "We should have woken her."

"Wake her now, and she's going to bite our heads off for letting her sleep through a goddamn UFO. Our best bet is to pretend we slept through it ourselves. We can all watch it for the first time when we hook up the videotape."

"Glad to see you haven't lost a step in your old age. You can still outthink a twelve-year-old."

Debbie gave him a shove, then sneaked back into the cocoonlike warmth of the jeep.

· · ·

"Cool fireworks, Daddy. But I thought it was illegal to shoot fireworks in the mountains."

Chuck sat next to Debbie on the foldout couch in the RV, his head in his hands, as he watched Ashley run her fingers over the glowing television screen, tracing the path of the lights as they rose up—in beautiful high definition—above the dunes.

There was no doubt about it, she was right. On the large screen they could clearly see that the balls of lights were nothing more than fireworks, amplified by the clear, dry, dark air, rising from some makeshift launch hidden somewhere beyond the dunes. Chuck didn't need to look at Debbie to know she was as disappointed as he was. He felt foolish, getting so excited about something as simple and common as fireworks. It didn't mean for certain that the lights they'd recorded from the watchtower had also been fireworks, but this time, they had clearly allowed their enthusiasm to get the best of them.

Another case of "locational suggestion," Chuck thought to himself. It happened all the time, even to experienced investigators. Go to a place known for a specific type of phenomenon—be it UFO sightings, Bigfoot, ghosts—and your mind was primed to play tricks. Bears became Sasquatch. Wind chimes became visions of the dead. And fireworks became UFOs.

"You're exactly right," Chuck finally said, masking his dissatisfaction. "There's a fire ban around here. We need to show this tape to the park ranger."

He got up from the couch and told Debbie to start preparing breakfast as he moved to grab the video camera that was attached to the TV. It wasn't just the reserve sheriff's deputy in him that spurred him out of the RV and across the short distance between the parking area and the ranger's cabin; he felt duped by whoever was launching fireworks in the middle of a fire zone. Nobody had been trying to hoax him. Hell, if anything, he and Debbie had hoaxed themselves, but it was just the sort of incident that would give Tammy ammunition the next time they argued over one of his planned excursions.

The last thing he needed was to give Tammy more reasons not to believe. She was the ultimate supportive wife, but sooner or later, he was going to push her too far. Every step he took away from finding evidence that would make her believe endangered the depth to which he could commit to his passion.

By the time he'd found the ranger behind her desk in the back corner of the rustic office, he was close to fuming. It didn't help that the ranger—shaped like a spark plug, with shoulders almost as broad as Chuck's and a haircut that was part bowl, part shovel—was immediately on the defensive, denying that any fireworks could have gone up in her territory without her knowing about it. But after he'd shown her the video, her demeanor had quickly changed. She assured him that someone was going to get in a lot of trouble, and that the video would be evidence enough for a serious fine, if not actual jail time.

Then she looked at him, a curious expression on her face.

"What were you doing filming out there in the middle of the night, anyway? Looking for mountain lions?"

"UFOs."

Without pause, Chuck explained to the ranger that he and his sister were UFO investigators. He told her about the lights they'd seen over Memorial Day, and how they had been hoping to confirm a sighting—but instead had seen only fireworks.

Considering her serious disposition, he'd expected a response somewhere between amusement and downright derision. Instead, she surprised him.

"Well, I've got a story for you," she said.

With that, she told him that a few months earlier, she'd gone out

on horseback one late afternoon to investigate a possible female griz-
zly death high in the mountains, behind the sand dunes—in the area
where Chuck and Debbie had seen the lights over Memorial Day. The
ranger had traveled farther back into the mountains than she had ever
been before, looking for the body of the bear, up on her horse. Suddenly, out of nowhere, a half dozen well-armed guys appeared. They
were all in camouflage, toting what appeared to be machine guns, and
they told her in no uncertain terms that this particular area was off-
limits.

Her horse neighed beneath her and shied away from the guys,
nearly sending her to the ground. But she'd come back at the camou-
flaged men angrily, telling them that she was a park ranger, that this
was park property, and that she had full authority. The men had responded that her authority ended a few hundred yards back—and they
had turned her horse around and forcefully escorted her the way she'd
come.

To this day, she'd never found out where the military personnel had
come from or what sort of base might have been hidden out there in
the mountains. Knowing the terrain, she didn't believe they had simply
hiked in and out; they'd had to have a more permanent campground in
the vicinity. But her higher-ups had simply told her to avoid that area in
the future.

Chuck listened to her story, wishing he'd had one of his notebooks
with him. He had to wonder—last night's lights were certainly fireworks, but the lights he and Debbie had seen over Memorial Day—
could they have had something to do with a secret military base in the
area?

Just as interesting was the thought that a park ranger could be
turned off park land by armed men in camouflage with no explanation.
The ranger was a federal agent, but they had escorted her away, at gun-
point.

You didn't need to be a conspiracy theorist to see that the real power wasn't in badges or official IDs. There were levels beneath levels.

Some secrets went back decades, and whether you went looking for them or just stumbled into them, the results could be just as dangerous.

# CHAPTER 17

33°37.38′N, 105°13.60′ W

"Chuck."

Chuck had his head down, his eyes focused on the GPS, his lungs struggling against desert air so filled with dust and sand that it was like breathing underwater, even filtered through the thick red-white-and-blue bandana that he had wrapped around the lower half of his sunburned face.

"Chuck!"

He refused to break his concentration. Debbie had been yelling his name for at least five minutes now, but he was determined to ignore her. They'd been out in the desert for at least three hours, the sun was like a nuclear bomb in the sky above him, and the back of his neck felt so hot it might as well have been in flames. But there was no way he was going to let Debbie pull his attention away from the GPS.

It was hard enough trying to read the numbers while simultaneously keeping an eye on the ground beneath his feet. He'd been walking in circles for at least twenty minutes—he was already recognizing shoots of dried scrub grass and the odd gnarled cactus—but the last thing he needed to do was stumble into a rattlesnake nest or kick over a rock hiding a scorpion. That would be a hell of a lot more trouble than being a little lost, even with his thick jeans tucked into his boots. He had a snakebite kit in his equipment pack, but he didn't want to try it out here, sixty miles north of nowhere.

"Chuck, goddamn it! Look up!"

With a grimace, he finally did. It took him an entire minute to locate Debbie from her voice, because she wasn't level with where he was kicking his way through the shrub-marked desert, she was fifteen feet up, standing on the top of a huge, jagged boulder. And she was smiling.

Debbie pointed at an aging, painted mark next to her on a portion of the rock that stuck up from the rest of it.

"I got tired of following you and just took off in a straight line. Guess what I found?"

"No fucking way," Chuck said.

Chuck ran toward her, forgetting about the heat, snakes, and sweat. Less than a minute later, he was up on the rock next to her, checking the GPS again. Sure enough, the red digital numbers blinked in tune to the digits written on the scrap of paper jammed in the pocket of his jeans. He'd memorized them on the long ride out into the desert from Roswell, and he was pretty sure he'd never forget them. Just the fact that he had those coordinates in his possession put him in a select group of maybe a dozen living people.

"You can see right down the mountain for miles. Down into the valley, right to the debris field."

Chuck stood next to her. She was right; from on top of the rock he had a direct, unobstructed view for what must have been thirty miles, desert and underbrush sloping downward all the way into what was once Mac Brazel's ranch land. Chuck held out the GPS, playing with the dials.

"It's a perfect line," he said.

The second set of coordinates, for a location that they intended to visit next, were a bit better known. In fact, they were the focal point of more than fifty years of frantic investigations: the crash site of the UFO: 33°56.35′N, 105°18.41′W.

Chuck had been told that the debris site was marked by a piece of PVC pipe jammed into the ground and an arrow painted into the sand. He wouldn't be walking in circles following the GPS when they got there; he'd be on his hands and knees, making good use of the Velcro pads they'd brought with them in their equipment packs.

"See the underbrush along the way, how it's grown back shorter than the areas on either side? See the knocked-down trees, right dead center leading all the way to the field?

"It's like something came right through, maybe even dragged along the ground, changing the growth patterns. Even after fifty years it's still something quite visible."

Chuck looked at Debbie and considered giving her a hug. The trip out to where they were now standing, known in UFO circles as the Ragsdale Site, had been challenging, even before the three-hour final hike through rattlesnake country. Twice, they'd had to go through breaks in aging fences meant to keep people like them out, and in some areas they'd nearly totaled his jeep trying to work their way over trails that would have pushed experienced ranch horses to their limits.

But the real obstacle hadn't been the terrain or the GPS; the real task had been getting the coordinates in the first place, something that Chuck might never have been able to accomplish on his own.

He'd come a long way since his first visit to Roswell with his family, from the days of just being another "tourist" with aliens on his brain. Over the years, he'd been back to Roswell—and the UFO Museum—so many times that everyone who worked there recognized him on sight. He'd met most of the living players in the Roswell story. He'd also gotten to know the museum's director and numerous other witnesses who'd been living in Roswell since the incident itself.

But it wasn't until his sister had joined him that things really started to click. It shouldn't have been any surprise to Chuck that Glenn Dennis and many of the other old-timers Chuck was getting to know would immediately have taken to his headstrong, pretty sister; but soon after meeting Debbie, Chuck's visits to the museum took on an almost collegial feel. Eventually, Dennis was taking them into the back office he kept at the museum, and showing them items that had come in that hadn't yet been put on display.

When Chuck had finally gotten up the nerve to ask the mortician for the exact coordinates to the debris site, he'd half expected Dennis to kick them back out into the tourists' pen. But the old man had smiled at Debbie, then rummaged in the top drawer of his desk. Not only had he given them the debris site, but he gave them the Ragsdale Site as well.

Chuck and Debbie had decided to visit Ragsdale first, because it was lesser known than Brazel's original debris field, and not coincidentally, harder to get to. In fact, there were three "crash" sites associated with the Roswell incident; the original debris site sixty miles northwest of Roswell, also known as "the Corona Site" because of its proximity to the small town of Corona; the "Corn Ranch Site," twenty miles north of Roswell; and Ragsdale, named after a truck driver named Jim Ragsdale who'd come forward with his own eyewitness account.

Ragsdale's story was one of the more vivid, if less than credible, accounts of the incident that had occurred that July Fourth weekend in 1947. In an affidavit signed in 1993, the trucker had claimed that on that night he and his girlfriend—a woman with the Hollywood-ready name Trudy Truelove—"were lying in the back of my pickup truck, buck naked, drinking beer and having a good ol' time when all hell broke loose." According to the affidavit, something saucer-shaped flew right over his head, then crashed, embedding itself in a nearby rock. Ragsdale and Truelove grabbed a flashlight and went to the crash site—finding a flying saucer with a big hole ripped in its side. He and Trudy left, but Ragsdale also claimed that the next morning, when he'd returned to try to salvage pieces of the craft, he'd seen bodies—"four or five feet long at most"—but before he could investigate further, military trucks showed up and scared him away.

Over the years, Ragsdale's account had been called into question by numerous skeptics. But many Roswell believers had taken to the idea of multiple impact sites—imagining a scenario in which a craft first made contact with the ground near Corona, depositing debris across Brazel's field, then rebounded into the air, depositing more pieces—and perhaps bodies—at either the Corn Site or Ragsdale.

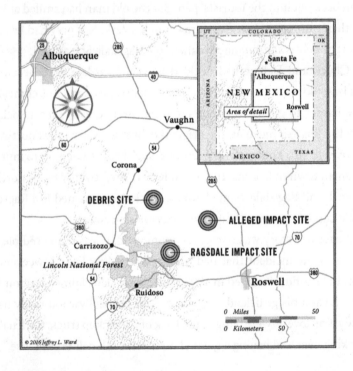

Standing next to Debbie up on the rock, Chuck noticed a huge crack running down one side. Maybe it was not big enough to have once held an embedded flying saucer, but it was certainly a traumatic-looking geological scar. As he looked out toward the same debris field, miles away, where Brazel had discovered silvery pieces of *something*, Chuck didn't care if Ragsdale had been telling the truth or concocting a monumental lie. More than the hundreds, if not thousands, of interviews they'd conducted, and the countless sites they had visited, in his mind, just by being there, up on that rock, he and Debbie had cemented themselves in the realm of UFOlogy as true professional investigators.

*Boots on the ground*, as their father might have put it, meant more than any number of files in a filing cabinet.

• • •

"That's a Gray. Definitely a Gray. And two Reptilians."

Chuck squinted through the windshield of his jeep at the shapes moving through the shadows of the poorly lit crosswalk in front of them. There was so much caked sand and dirt on the glass from the long drive back from the debris site that it was hard to see much. Besides, Debbie had always had the better vision of the two.

"Where, I don't see the Gray."

"Behind the Klingon," Debbie said. "And is that Chewbacca? Or a very obese Ewok?"

Chuck flashed the brights, causing the shapes to freeze in the center of the road. The Chewbacca made a gesture that might have had something to do with the Force—or maybe more to do with the forty-ounce beer bottle he was sharing with one of the Reptilians.

"Christ, where do these people find the time to make these costumes?"

"Come on, Chuck. You know you're dying to bust out your *Battlestar Galactica* flight suit. We've still got plenty of time. From what I've heard, the ball goes all night."

Chuck doused the brights, letting the revelers in the street ahead of them stumble back into the shadows. Debbie's joking aside, neither of them would have been caught dead at the Alien Dress Up Ball, no matter how late it was supposed to run. Chuck didn't begrudge the tourists their fun, but the last way he wanted to spend a Saturday night in Roswell, over the July Fourth weekend no less, was dancing with his sister in a hall filled with people even geekier than himself.

Once the costumed gaggle had passed, Chuck gunned the engine and quickly navigated the jeep toward the outskirts of town. They'd already spent the hour since they'd made it back from the desert scouting out the best spot to spend the night, and they'd found what might be the perfect lookout, a parking area high enough to give them a good view of the mountains, facing the same sky where the air force radar operators had once first begun tracking a strange, unidentified object moving erratically into a storm.

Once they parked the jeep, they set up camp: cameras, telescopes, recording equipment, and their night-vision goggles, everything they'd need in case history wanted to repeat itself. Even though the night turned out to be uneventful, they were still so amped by the day's hike through the two crash sites that they didn't break camp until well after 3:00 a.m.

The next morning, their last in Roswell before heading back to their respective homes, they decided on one last trip to the museum. They'd planned on listening to a visiting speaker, but when they arrived, a small crowd was in the front entrance. Chuck immediately recognized the two men at the center of the crowd: Tom Carey and Don Schmitt, two of the more famous Roswell investigators, who between them had written a number of books on the subject and appeared on various TV shows over the years.

A young man, a teenager, probably seventeen, was showing the two investigators a Polaroid of a mutilated cow. Chuck couldn't help himself and quickly moved close enough so that he could overhear the conversation.

The teenager was telling Carey and Schmitt that he'd seen a triangular craft the night before, right over the lookout where Chuck and Debbie had been parked, and that the craft had dropped the cow and sped off.

Chuck just smiled to himself. The kid must be trying to get famous or maybe land on TV. Between the Sci-Fi Channel, Discovery, Science, and even the History Channel, there were so many late-night hours to fill that producers were practically giving specials away to anyone with good visuals and a story to tell. But Debbie, with her MUFON credentials, wasn't the type to let something like that go.

As the teenager walked away, leaving the Polaroid with Carey and Schmitt, Debbie stepped forward.

"Sorry, guys, that's a nice picture of a dead cow, but that kid's story is bull."

Carey was still looking at the Polaroid, but Schmitt turned toward Debbie.

"How do you know that?"

"We were out in that exact spot all night. No kids, no cow, no craft. It's a hoax."

Carey glanced up from the Polaroid.

"Do I recognize you guys?"

"You might," Chuck said. "We're independent investigators. Well, I'm an independent investigator. My sister is with MUFON."

"Brother and sister? That might be a first."

Carey smiled. After they all gave more detailed introductions, Carey surprised Chuck with an invitation.

"You guys interested in helping us out with a project we're working on at the debris site? A month from now an archaeological dig, actually. And it's going to be on TV."

Chuck didn't mention that he and his sister had just spent the day before checking out the same location. He was too busy trying to figure out what he was going to tell his boss to get himself out of work for the necessary time commitment, and more difficult yet, how he was going to sell the excursion to Tammy. He couldn't afford any more furniture for the kitchen without getting rid of some of his equipment. And from what Carey and Schmitt were telling him, he was going to need everything he owned to keep up with these Roswell experts.

But Tammy would have to understand. Two days ago, Chuck had seen the debris site only on a map. Yesterday, he'd trekked through it on his own two boots.

A month from now, he was going to be digging for alien artifacts on national TV.

# CHAPTER 18

## CORONA DEBRIS SITE,
## SUMMER 2002

Late afternoon, the temperature touching 110 degrees, knees down in a pit of packed sand more than three feet deep, sweat soaking through the back of his shirt, gloved hands around the hilt of a trowel, strangling the damn thing like it was a murderous rattler, Chuck was damn near about to explode. He hadn't been this frustrated or angry in as long as he could remember, and the only thing that was keeping him from leaping out of the hole and heading right for the archaeologist in charge—Dr. Bill Doleman, head of the archaeology department at the University of New Mexico and a well-respected, twenty-two-year veteran of numerous celebrated digs—was Chuck's sister, in the sand next to him, whispering that the cameras were still rolling.

Looking up from the trowel, Chuck could see that she was right; the two cameramen were still standing by the yellow tape that cordoned off the dig site, holding those huge, bazookalike television cameras over their shoulders. The two union men couldn't have looked more bored, and Chuck didn't blame them. Even though the cordoned-off area was within long visual range of the PVC pipe marking the debris coordinates, and the Sci-Fi Channel had provided Doleman and his team of a dozen volunteers—mostly archaeology students, with a handful of UFO enthusiasts like Chuck and Debbie scattered about—with enough equipment to conduct a solid dig, Chuck considered what was going on an utter farce.

He felt duped, and Debbie felt the same way. Despite what Carey and Schmitt had told them—not just in person, but in a series of encrypted emails over the past month describing the archaeology project and the show they were going to host—Chuck and Debbie weren't actually helping to conduct a bona-fide search for artifacts from the 1947 crash. The cameras weren't recording them in case they found something that would change the world. They were kneeling there, in those dusty pits, baking under the sun, for *background*.

Ignoring the directions he had been given by one of the producers, who was off in some air-conditioned motor home out of camera view, Chuck lifted his head high enough out of the pit so he could see where Don Schmitt and Tom Carey were standing, in the midst of giving an interview—right in front of a helicopter, rotors spinning. The main camera—the one that would be in focus—was up close and centered on the two men, while the two cameramen nearest Chuck were simply panning back and forth. Chuck shook his head.

If it had only been about the screen time, Chuck wouldn't have cared; he wasn't trying to get famous by going on the archaeology dig. He had sincerely hoped to find something. That's how he had gotten Tammy's permission to join the project in the first place; he'd told her that this was the first real chance anyone had had in years to conduct a scientific investigation at the Roswell crash site. Paid for by a national network, run by a professional archaeologist, this was a chance Chuck couldn't pass over.

Besides feeling that they'd been brought there under false pretenses, Chuck believed that the dig itself was a farce.

"This is ridiculous," he said, breaking another of the producer's commandments by speaking. "This is goddamn dinosaur dirt."

Debbie stifled a laugh. She understood exactly what he meant, because he'd been yelling about it since breakfast, when he'd first read the directions handed out by Doleman and the production crew. From the start, they'd been told to dig pits of seventy centimeters, two feet, and more. Chuck knew from his experience with archaeology at the Raven site, two feet meant they were digging millions of years into the past. The crash at Roswell had occurred in 1947. It didn't take an archaeology professor to know that what they were doing was mimicking a dig for the cameras. What they should have been doing was strip digging in tiny increments, one or two centimeters at a time, and not shoveling pits.

Chuck wasn't the only one getting upset at the situation; all day, murmurs had been spreading through the ranks of volunteers. A few had already walked off set, because of the heat, and at least one had quit when a cameraman had told him that his digging was causing too much noise, interrupting the interviews. Aside from Chuck, another of the volunteers who seemed closest to the breaking point had been complaining bitterly to anyone who would listen about the conditions and the purposelessness of the background players since breakfast. Since he had been silently digging two pits down from Chuck and Debbie for the better part of the last two hours, Chuck thought maybe he had finally resigned himself to the situation—but suddenly, a loud grunt let Chuck know that things were about to get much uglier.

Chuck turned just in time to see him leaping out of his pit and rushing straight for the two investigators, who were now climbing into the helicopter.

Chuck watched the man go by, shouting "I'm going to kill that son of a bitch," then glanced at his sister. If he hadn't been a cop, he might have given it another minute. Instead, he dropped his trowel and was up and out of his pit, legs pumping as he closed the distance.

He reached him just as the man seemed to be reaching for Schmitt's throat, prepared, it seemed, to drag him out of the helicopter. Chuck wrapped his arms around his shoulders, pried him loose, then yelled at Schmitt to take off. With a burst of strength, he pulled the infuriated man back, and together they watched the chopper rise as fast as the pilot could manage.

As he yelled to a nearby production assistant to get some cold water and a wet towel to help calm the man, he realized that everyone had a breaking point. And if he didn't do something soon, he'd be the one doing the throttling. The way things were going, he wasn't sure any of the other volunteers would have been willing to try to stop him.

*   *   *

It was well past midnight by the time the argument spilled out into the parking lot of the kitschy Mexican restaurant in a poorly lit alley, kitty-corner to Main Street, downtown Roswell. Professor Doleman was shouting loud enough to compete with the clatter from the restaurant's overtaxed kitchen, his pointing finger inches from Chuck's face, as Chuck backed down the steps that led between a pair of huge, lime-green garbage bins and a delivery truck with a massive yellow sombrero emblazoned on the hood.

Debbie was a step behind Doleman, ready to jump between the men if the heated words became something more, but Chuck could hardly see her through the red sparks floating in front of his eyes. He had simply wanted to give the archaeologist a piece of his mind before he and Debbie walked off the dig, but somewhere between the tortilla chips appetizer and the fajita-based main course, the dialogue had turned confrontational. Chuck had found himself asking if the Ph.D. was being purposely obstinate, or if he was just plain stupid, and from there it had only gotten worse. By the time the restaurant manager had asked them to finish their discussion outside, Chuck had crossed so many lines he would not have been surprised if the esteemed professor had started throwing fists.

"Twenty-two years," the man was shouting, his finger piercing the air in front of Chuck's eyes. "I've been conducting digs for twenty-two years and you're going to question my methods?"

"I don't care how many years you've been doing this. That doesn't make what's going on out here any less idiotic."

Chuck held up his own hands, showing the man the blisters that had formed on most of his fingers from the trowel. Then the backs of his arms, which were sunburned and caked in sand.

"We're out there eating dust, and for what? You know better than I do that we're digging into the Stone Age. Seventy centimeters? Are we looking for a UFO or a T Rex?"

Doleman didn't argue further, as the door to the restaurant slammed shut behind Debbie, cutting out the din from the kitchen and leaving them alone in the parking lot.

"This is what the producers want. It's TV, it's got to look a certain way."

Chuck understood Doleman's conflict. Just being part of the Roswell investigation must have been a difficult decision for the professor; scientists who attached themselves to anything remotely connected to UFO studies were quickly given derogatory labels and often mocked by their colleagues. Many conspiracy theorists believed that it was actually part of a fairly sophisticated system meant to keep anyone from looking too hard at the related phenomena. For the most part, scientists who wanted to remain respected in their fields couldn't look into UFOs, which meant that the only people willing to delve into the subject were those who were already on the fringes. Doleman was certainly not a fringe player, but he was walking a fine line, trying to maintain a level of respectability while playing expert on a Roswell-focused show.

But Chuck sensed that the man might be willing to let him do more than provide background shots.

"The crash occurred in 1947. If we were to try to find something from that year, how deep would we need to go?"

The archaeologist didn't need to think to come up with the answer.

"Ten centimeters."

"And based on the erosion patterns since 1947, the runoffs from various storms, and the effects of the heat and winds, do you have an idea where any debris material might have settled, if we could start from the exact crash coordinates from July of '47?"

Doleman put his glasses back on.

"I might have a few ideas."

"Then I'll make a deal with you. Let me and my sister stay an extra day after the shoot ends and conduct a strip dig. Ten foot by two foot, at the proper depth, at the right place."

The archaeologist seemed surprised that Chuck even knew what a strip dig was; maybe he couldn't picture a sheriff's deputy crawling around an Anasazi pueblo with his wife on an anniversary trip or a UFO nut who knew how to properly use a sifter.

"You're serious. You're going to come out on your own time, in the heat, on your own and do this? No cameras?"

Chuck nodded. Doleman thought for a moment.

"We break set tomorrow morning. The rest of the crew and volunteers will be cleaning up the camp, but if I see you out at the meeting point at six a.m., ready to go, I'll take you out to do a proper dig."

Six o'clock. Less than five hours away. Chuck could tell the man didn't seriously think he and his sister would be willing to take him up on the offer. But he obviously didn't know Chuck or Debbie. Given the opportunity, they would have jumped in the jeep that minute and driven up a Class 9 trail to have a legitimate shot at the debris site.

"Tomorrow morning," Chuck said, slapping a blistered hand against the hood of the delivery truck, smack in the middle of the sombrero. "We do it the right way. And if we find anything, it won't be a goddamn dinosaur."

•   •   •

"Oh my god," Debbie whispered, as she leaned over the pan of fresh dirt. Her face was pale, her cheeks constricted tight against the bones. Her gloved hand was on Chuck's shoulder, and he could feel the way her muscles trembled beneath her denim work shirt.

"Do you see that?"

Chuck still had his trowel between his hands, about to push through another centimeter down. From his angle he could barely see into the pan, but even so, he could clearly see the metallic glint flashing out from somewhere in the thick brown dirt. Still, his mind refused to believe that it could be anything more than a trick of light. Four hours under the hot sun, after so few hours of sleep—how could it be anything else?

Even so, the adrenaline rose inside him as he let the shovel fall to the sand. A moment later he was on his knees next to Debbie. She carefully reached into the pan and used two fingers to lift the glittering thing out of the dirt.

The object was thin, silvery, and triangular, about the width of a quarter. Even as she lifted it off the ground, the corners started to curl inward, perhaps reacting to the heat from the sun or the pressure of her fingers, but the material seemed resilient, as strong as metal, as thin as it was.

"I don't know what it is," Chuck said. "But I think we need to get Dr. Doleman."

Chuck looked back over his shoulder, trying to spot the archaeologist. The area where they were now digging was much more desolate than the location from the day before; other than their ten-foot-long strip area, designated by wooden stakes they had placed at precise points Doleman had measured out for them, connected by strips of white tape and lengths of string, there wasn't much out there beyond a few boulder-sized rocks, some grass, a smattering of clumps of dried brush, and lots of sand. Even so, Doleman was hard to spot, having strolled a dozen yards back to talk to Tom Carey in the shade of a low outcropping.

Chuck had been pleasantly surprised to find Doleman much more amiable and acquiescent when they had met at the truck stop by base camp six hours earlier. As Chuck had guessed, Doleman was surprised that they'd shown up. But he kept his end of the bargain and drove them out to the debris site, using the coordinates that Chuck had gotten from the mortician, which jibed with his own set of coordinates, garnered from the UFO Museum for the Sci-Fi Channel shoot. As soon as they'd arrived at the PVC pipe marker, Chuck had again pulled what he called his "Mr. Spock" on the professor.

"Given everything we know from witness statements from weather patterns and wind erosion, what is your best guess as to where the debris from a crash might have traveled in the past sixty years?"

Since the night before, Doleman had made some calculations and come up with an answer, so he led Chuck and Debbie on a quarter-mile hike. Along the way, he used his hands to pantomime streams of water that might have run through the desert from various notable storms, and the effects of the wind against different elevations and dunes.

Eventually, they'd reached a best-guess location, a stretch of desert spotted with clumps of desert grasses, sloping downward in the general direction of Roswell.

Immediately, Chuck and Debbie had cordoned off an area for their strip dig, using string and tape to delineate ten-foot strips, separated into two-foot segments. Then they'd retrieved as much equipment as they could carry from the Sci-Fi Channel production—sifters, buckets, pans, shovels—and had gone to work. In short order, they'd scraped away a ten-centimeter level of grass and sand, revealing the fresh dirt beneath.

The first thing Chuck had done, once they'd dug to the proper depth, was to get down on his hands and knees and touch the dirt with his cheek—causing Debbie to smile and Doleman to look at him as if he was insane. Maybe she understood; at least a part of Chuck was back in 1947, right there that night when something came careening down out of the sky, crashing with enough force to spread metallic debris across an entire field.

Then Debbie had joined him on the ground, and together they'd begun to work the strip, just as he and Tammy had learned to do at the Raven site, carefully sifting the dirt, inch by inch.

Debbie Ziegelmeyer

Debbie Ziegelmeyer

The blisters, the sunburn, the heat, none of this bothered Chuck now that he was doing this the right way. It didn't matter that he probably wouldn't find anything; at least he was now involved in a proper investigation. That, to him, was the high; flashing back to every UFO sighting he'd researched, every animal mutilation he'd studied—it wasn't finding answers that gave him that thrill, it was searching for them—applying scientific methods to something that seemed to defy science.

And then, suddenly, Debbie had gone quiet next to him, when she had, in fact, found something.

She held the metallic triangle higher, and they watched how the breeze seemed to pull at the material, threatening to send it floating right out of her hand. It shone like a bit of polished Mylar.

"It's so light. But it doesn't feel like foil."

The material resembled what Mac Brazel and Jesse Marcel had described when interviewed by Roswell investigators, such as the nuclear physicist Stanton Friedman, as well as Carey and Schmitt.

Since Doleman was still out of earshot, Chuck quickly found a plastic specimen bag. He and Debbie carefully placed the triangular piece into the bag, sealing it tight. Then together they rushed to where Doleman and Carey were still deep in conversation.

Chuck interrupted the two men, and Doleman let Debbie undo the seal of the bag. Together the four of them took turns peering at the glimmering object. Eventually, Doleman held it between his fingers and an envelope, trying to get a better look.

"I don't know what it is," Doleman said. "It's not naturally occurring, but other than that, it could be anything."

"Certainly interesting," Carey said. "Tag it and bag it."

To Chuck's surprise, Carey started walking toward the truck that had brought them out to the field. But Doleman still seemed sufficiently intrigued by the object.

"Take a few pictures first. Then we'll give it a number and send it to the University of New Mexico with whatever else was found during the dig."

Debbie Ziegelmeyer

Doleman handed the object back to Debbie, who slipped it back into the specimen bag. As Doleman walked away, leaving them alone with their discovery, Chuck tried to comprehend why Doleman and Carey seemed to be missing the significance of the moment.

Doleman was an archaeologist, and he was used to digging up ancient objects that could be easily categorized and identified, matched to ancient texts, earlier digs, and history books. Carey had been to Roswell so many times, interviewed so many people, that a tiny fragment of something, no matter how interesting it seemed, wasn't going to raise his heart rate beyond its regular thud.

Maybe Chuck was too willing to believe, but in his mind, the object he and Debbie had just uncovered was the first real artifact that, at least observationally, appeared similar to the debris Brazel had found and turned over to the U.S. military almost sixty years ago.

To Chuck, this was real, physical evidence.

Looking at Debbie, he could tell she was thinking the same thing. The question was—what was the appropriate next step?

Chuck was still a sheriff's deputy with a day job. His interest in UFOs was certainly now more than a hobby, but this felt much bigger than everything that had come before.

Hell, he'd been searching so long, he wasn't sure what he was supposed to do now that he had actually found something.

# CHAPTER 19

## NATIONAL INSTITUTE FOR DISCOVERY SCIENCE HEADQUARTERS, LAS VEGAS, NEVADA, 2003

The creature was enormous. Three hundred pounds at least, nearly six feet tall at its haunches, layers of rippling muscle visible beneath its thick black fur. Even from a distance of twenty yards, it stank of burning sulfur, and as it moved through the trees it seemed to affect the air around it, emanating waves of some sort of odd static, rustling the nearby leaves and warping the tree limbs as if they were being pressed back by some invisible force field.

As the creature came closer, its form was described, variously, as a giant wolf or wildcat. Other witnesses in other places described it as bipedal and vaguely humanoid, somewhere between a bear and an ape. Its demeanor was both natural and unnatural; it moved like an animal, testing the air with its snout and tongue, clawing at tree bark or pawing at the ground, but it couldn't be caught or harmed. Bullets either bounced off its hide or went right through it. Some witnesses described it coming out of a luminescent tunnel that appeared a few feet off the ground. Others first saw it appear beneath a flying object—a saucer, a black triangle, or a cigar-shaped craft.

However the creature appeared, it was decidedly malevolent. It left its signature in mutilated cattle and horses, some mangled so badly it took hours to find all their limbs and body parts. According to the reports, the creature didn't harm humans, but according to the Native American tribes that populated the area that the creature seemed to call home, if you dared look the creature directly in its cold blue eyes, it would take your soul.

Robert Bigelow, fifty-nine, lowered the open file onto the desk in his office at the National Institute for Discovery Science, on the second floor of an unremarkable two-story building near the Las Vegas Strip, and leaned back in his chair. The story of the creature was told in a nearly sixty-page document—filled with first-person accounts, scientific data including infrared signatures, EMF readings, and soil samples, and mostly inconclusive photos. Page after page of corroborating witness statements were as frustrating as they were terrifying. Cattle-mutilating monsters, Native American mythological horror stories, interdimensional tunnels, UFOs—no matter how many eyewitnesses his team had interviewed, no matter how many strange data points they collected or electromagnetic readings they got—the crazy factor was just too damn high. No mainstream publication, scientific or otherwise, was going to consider a study like this as anything more than science fiction. No mainstream scientist, outside of the open-minded group Bigelow had gathered together to staff his brainchild, NIDS, was going to risk career suicide to even look into such a story, no matter what evidence Bigelow's team could produce.

Hell, Bigelow himself was having trouble keeping his eyes from rolling as he dug through the report, and he knew, better than anyone, that many phenomena that appeared fictional actually had scientific explanations. Futuristic technology could appear like magic or myth to the uninitiated.

He'd come a long way since his childhood, when he'd witnessed nuclear testing from his bedroom window in New Mexico, but he could still see that incredible blast of light, that mushroom cloud rising into the predawn sky. If he hadn't known what he'd been looking at, God knows what he might have thought it was. And wasn't a nuclear explosion as incredible as an animal mutilation, or some sort of creature stalking a ranch in Ute Indian country, near the southern Utah border?

Then again, Bigelow hadn't founded the NIDS to study Native American mythology. His team had found its way to Skinwalker Ranch, in Uintah County, next to the Ute Indian Reservation, almost by accident. Even the NIDS itself was somewhat tangential to what Bigelow was hoping to achieve.

His journey to the nondescript, two-story building in the shadow of the lavish, neon-infused Strip casinos—the giant Pyramid, the battling pirate ships, the Romanesque palaces—read like a classic American Dream narrative. Through hard work, a little luck, and a lot of timing, he'd turned a small investment in rental properties into a massive real estate empire. His dozens of apartment buildings and motels had morphed into Budget Suites of America in 1988. As Vegas suddenly exploded as the prime tourist destination in the country, Bigelow's fortune magnified, making him one of the richest men in Nevada. But real estate had only been a means to an end. Since childhood, Bigelow had hidden his real intentions from everyone around him. Not even his wife knew his secret goal—because it had seemed so extreme, so impossible, he hadn't dared put it into words. But now he was a billionaire and he could do pretty much what he wanted.

His secret had its origins around the same time he was witnessing the nuclear tests from his bedroom. He'd begun to hear stories, more fantastic than the mushroom clouds, from family members, especially his grandparents. The stories were about extraordinary sightings—and one defining incident that Bigelow would later learn to categorize as a C1 encounter.

"What they saw," he'd one day tell a newspaper reporter about his parents as the reporter compiled an obligatory bio after one of Bigelow's larger real estate deals, "was an object that they thought was an airplane on fire at first. They stopped the car. It was nighttime and the object was coming right for them. And it grew bigger and bigger. In a very short time, a matter of maybe seconds, until it filled up the windshield. Then they realized it wasn't an airplane on fire; they didn't know what it was. Their car was stopped on the side of the road in a remote location at night—and they thought they were dead, until, at the last second before impact, it made a right-angle turn and zipped out of sight. And I remember how shook up they were. Even in telling me years later, they had a very serious look on their faces" (Amy Standon, *Salon*, June 7, 2001, "My Own Private Space Station").

The story was no different from the thousands of other sightings reported by the newspapers of Bigelow's childhood—but this was personal, this was family. And Bigelow had become possessed by the belief that the distance between man and space was not insurmountable. If visitors from somewhere in the vastness of space had indeed been to Earth, mankind would find a way to reverse the trip.

To Bigelow, this was not fantasy. He was a practical thinker, educated in an era when American success was predicated on its reliance on science, engineering, and free, creative thought. His goal was to approach space travel, and the potential for extraterrestrial life, as an engineering problem.

Bigelow's real estate empire would be a means to an end. As soon as he felt capable of beginning his quest in earnest, he dedicated his wealth to creating a scientific understanding of unearthly possibilities. On the mainstream side of the coin, he'd endowed a new physics lab at the University of Nevada and added an additional $3.7 million "for the creation and continuation of a program that would attract to the university renowned experts on aspects of human consciousness." Going further, he'd funded a leading parapsychologist as the "Bigelow Chair" at the university, to study "altered states of consciousness, near-death experiences, and extrasensory perception."

From there, Bigelow's ambitions had led him in 1996 to launch the NIDS, an interdisciplinary organization made up of the top researchers in the fields of biology, geology, astrophysics, and chemistry, as well as trained former police detectives and FBI agents, tasked with studying verifiable UFO sightings. After Project Blue Book, the multiyear, official air force investigation into UFOs, NIDS was the first organized, well-funded attempt to approach the subject scientifically. NIDS established a twenty-four-hour hotline for citizens to report UFO sightings, and they received more than five thousand calls and emails over a two-year period. Teams of investigators were sent out into the field, using equipment that cost tens of thousands of dollars, from spectrophotometers to analyze strange lights in the sky to the best available night-vision recording devices.

Bigelow's goal, with NIDS, was simply to try to give the vast number of anomalies that were being reported the scientific attention they deserved. He wasn't trying to find UFOs, he was trying to use science to identify whatever it was people were seeing. He aimed to turn the UFOs into IFOs—Identified Flying Objects. But no matter how many Ph.D.s he coaxed to the two-story building in Vegas, he faced an uphill battle for anything resembling respect from the greater scientific community or the mainstream press. Colm Kelleher, the noted biochemist and cancer researcher he brought in to be NIDS's deputy administrator, had put it succinctly in an article with *Business Insider*: "The vast majority of scientists dismiss this type of research as being absolutely worthless. . . . There's a real aura of ridicule and trivialization surrounding the UFO field which makes scientists run a mile the other way. To many scientists, studying UFOs is really a career killer, and that hasn't changed in 50 years."

Looking through the file on his desk, Bigelow could understand the reluctance of the scientific community. This supernatural wolf-cat-bear-ape was right out of science fiction. But even the more common sightings—C1 encounters, like his own family's experiences—were regarded with ridicule, no matter how many witnesses there were. An entire town could call in reports, including police officers, military radar operators, politicians—and most scientists refused to publicly comment on any review of the data.

Bigelow often asked his team at NIDS what it would take to prove that something real was going on. If a saucer landed on the White House lawn, half of the country would call it a government conspiracy, the other half, a case of mass hysteria.

To be taken more seriously, NIDS focused on the cases that had a clear possibility of verifiable results. Sightings with multiple witnesses, involving scenarios that might lead to physical evidence. Through this methodology, they'd achieved some unique success. Bigelow believed that his team had identified the source of at least one of the more frequent types of sightings: Big Black Deltas, usually reported as giant, black triangles in the sky that seemed to hover, maneuver quickly, and accelerate to unusual speeds. Using sophisticated mapping techniques, NIDS scientists had shown a correlation between the sightings and the locations of known air force bases that were conducting research into "lighter-than-air" craft.

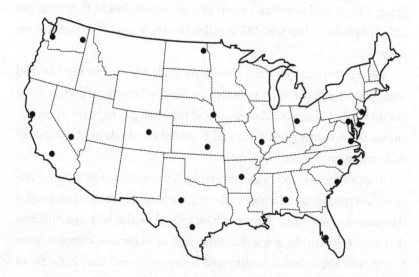

Employing an aircraft design specialist, and using military sources, the NIDS had concluded that the Deltas were most likely experimental blimps, powered by electrokinetic engines that had been under development by the air force since the early eighties.

Bigelow considered the revelation a clear success for the NIDS's methodology, even though the official press releases on the subject barely edged into the mainstream media. His team of Ph.D.s continued to focus on the more "provable" anomalies, but every now and then, the more extreme anomalous phenomena, such as cattle mutilations, were difficult to ignore.

Thousands of reported and unexplained individual instances of cattle mutilations had first led Bigelow and his team to a ranch in Utah. Bigelow considered most cattle-mutilation scenes outside the NIDS's charter, as the mutilations usually occurred without witnesses, and little physical evidence was left behind aside from the bodies. But the reports from Utah were staggering. Two different sets of ranch owners—and a large number of nearby witnesses—had been tormented by strange phenomena, from animal mutilations and UFO sightings to crop circles and flying orbs, as well as vivid accounts of huge, bizarre beasts that appeared out of nowhere, in line with "Skinwalker" mythologies of the local Native American tribes.

Rather than simply send a team to study the ranch, Bigelow had bought the damn place, for roughly two hundred thousand dollars. He'd put up fences to keep out the public and then had placed three of his scientists in permanent residence and provided hundreds of thousands of dollars in sophisticated equipment.

Though the research was continuing, his scientists—including a veterinarian specialist and a physicist—had witnessed numerous anomalies themselves. These ranged from sudden animal mutilations—mutilations that occurred within a few hundred feet of observers, minutes after they'd seen the animals healthy and unmarred—and scorch marks in the fields to UFO and "beastly" sightings, but for whatever reason, the recording devices had not yet picked up anything conclusive. Although there were many paranormal theories about what was going on at the ranch, ranging from portals into different dimensions, to extraterrestrial involvement, to some sort of secretive military testing, Bigelow had little more "evidence" than the very bizarre case report on his desk. A journalist connected to the NIDS would eventually publish the report in book form, but because of the subject matter, it would barely register in the mainstream. Bigelow's team had begun investigating another location at the center of numerous similar anomalies near Dulce, New Mexico. Some of his scientists believed these had clearer connections to some sort of secretive or military project, perhaps involving underground facilities.

Bigelow himself was taking constant risks with his reputation and wanted his primary focus to remain on phenomena that had the potential to yield scientific evidence. Skinwalkers made for vivid stories, but only pushed the scientific community further away from the study of UFOs. Numerous articles had already sprung up on the Internet about the reclusive billionaire who was spending his fortune searching for UFOs. Rumors in the UFO community were that he was either in league with the CIA or some other black ops government agency, involved in covering up proof of alien visitations to Earth, or using alien technology to further his own corporate empire. All because he was using his own money to try to involve the scientific community in what he believed to be a scientific quest.

Bigelow was willing to take risks. He firmly believed that future generations would look at the current belief system as ignorant and egocentric. The lack of acceptance of outer-worldly phenomena, in the face of a staggering number of witness accounts and radar evidence—page after page of radar data clearly showing unidentified blips, from Roswell to radar tracking Foo Fighters during World War II to the numerous UFO sightings near nuclear bases all over the world—was akin to primitive beliefs that the world was flat. When history was written in the future, it would consider UFOlogy the greatest ball the fourth estate had ever dropped.

The NIDS was just the beginning. Bigelow had a billion dollars at his disposal, and he planned to use his fortune to close the distance between UFOs and IFOS, unexplained anomalies and scientific explanations—and eventually, even Earth and space.

# CHAPTER 20

Chuck wasn't built for corporate espionage. It wasn't that he didn't have the brains for it; both his police training and his UFO work had made him adept at recognizing and obtaining valuable evidence, often at what he perceived to be high risk to himself. Nor was he lacking the expertise. In his day job, he'd worked in numerous corporate hives—from large, multinational engineering corporations to small, mom-and-pop chip-designing outfits.

The problem was that, physically, he wasn't built for the spy game. Physically, he was too damn big. Even now, with his wide shoulders pulled in tight, his head down, his knees bent as low as they could go toward the puke-green carpet that ran down the narrow aisle between the bank of stark white cubicles, he felt like a Harley in a china shop; or more accurately, an athletically built man in a black Harley sweatshirt trying to sneak through a semiconductor design plant. It didn't help that the tech engineer he was following down the corridor between the cubicles was a bit of a spectacle himself, wearing thick, gogglelike glasses, and a mustard-yellow Captain Kirk *Star Trek* T-shirt that was at least two sizes too small.

But if any of the other engineers or various support staff gathered in the football-field-sized rabbit warren of dry-wall cubes and aluminum-framed equipment cabinets noticed their progress, none of them seemed to have cared enough to give them a second look.

To be fair, it was midway through most of the engineering staff's lunch break, and most of the support staff knew Chuck, at least by sight. He wasn't technically an employee of the firm anymore, but his role as an independent contractor allowed him some level of access to the design floor. Although his current mission had nothing to do with semiconductors or the kind of work he did for the company that earned him just enough—combined with Tammy's two salaries from the two service industry jobs she'd been forced to take as he'd focused more of his time on his investigations—to cover their monthly expenses.

"You sure this is okay?" he whispered to the tech in the *Star Trek* shirt as he led him past the last set of cubicles and unlocked an unmarked door at the back of the vast room. "I wouldn't want to get you into any trouble."

The tech pulled the door open and ushered Chuck into a small engineering lab lined with cluttered shelves and state-of-the-art workstations. Fluorescent lighting panels flickered on above their heads, casting the chrome and plastic equipment in an eerie yellow glow.

"Are you kidding? And miss a chance at ending up in some CIA, black ops prison?" the man said with a grin. Chuck had a feeling he was only partly kidding. He had met enough conspiracy theorists to know he had hit the jackpot with this one, entirely by accident. A happy accident, he thought to himself, as the tech pointed to a large piece of sophisticated machinery in the far corner of the lab.

"Besides," the tech said, "if anyone catches us in here I'll tell them it's a calibration exercise. Wouldn't even really be a lie. Sometimes I use specimens from my rock collection to reset the EMS values. This specimen might be a little more unusual than some flecks of quartz I picked up on a camping trip to Joshua Tree, but it isn't going to blow up the microscope."

Then he eyed the manila envelope Chuck had under his right arm.

"Or is it?"

"According to the Sci-Fi Channel and the head of archaeology at the University of New Mexico, it's the plastic backing from a piece of duct tape."

The tech smiled.

"Good. As far as I know, duct tape never blew up an electron microscope."

They shared a moment of silence as they approached the machinery. Chuck didn't know the conspiracy-minded tech very well; he'd only met the man a few times during his work as a contractor, and aside from a love of science fiction, they might not have had all that much in common. But they both certainly agreed on one thing: Neither of them thought the specimen in Chuck's manila envelope was the backing of a piece of duct tape.

Before Chuck had first approached the tech in the Agilent cafeteria, he had gone through various stories in his head. He could have told the man that he needed help with a work project involving an unidentified piece of material. He could have made up some story about a scavenger hunt, or his police work, or a contest.

Instead, he'd settled on the truth. *See, I found this piece of strange material at the Roswell dig site, and I was wondering if you could help me find an electron microscope to take a closer look.* From the man's appearance, Chuck might have been able to guess that the tech was a believer in UFOs. He hadn't counted on the man's instant enthusiasm for the mission, or his willingness to break a few rules to get them access to the expensive piece of equipment.

As they reached the machine, the tech went to work powering up the control board. Chuck knew from his own work that the quarter-million-dollar scanning electron microscope could produce high-resolution images of any fragment of material that it was trained on—down to the micron—as well as an elemental identification from the periodic table. Agilent engineers used the SEM to examine the topography of integrated circuits, often to help find bugs in individual transistors. The machine was expensive to build and it cost money to operate. On his own, Chuck would never have been able to afford an examination session.

After he and Debbie had pulled the fragment out of the dig site, he'd spent months going back and forth with Doleman and the production staff from the Sci-Fi Channel shoot, trying to get them to run a real analysis on the object. He was shocked by their reluctance to go further than their quick, visual assessments. Eventually, he'd been able to convince Doleman to let him have the artifact back—on loan from the university's storage facilities—for his own analysis. The electron microscope seemed the best next step, and he'd begun trolling the Agilent cafeteria for the right set of hands. He'd been lucky to stumble on a tech willing to try to make history, even if the man had mentioned "black helicopters" more than once on the journey through the cubicles to the equipment lab. Chuck had stifled the urge to correct him; it wasn't the black helicopters that bothered Chuck, it was the SUVs.

Once the tech had the control console powered up, he shot a meaningful glance at the envelope. Chuck removed a pair of rubber gloves from his pocket and carefully retrieved the artifact, placing it on the scanning microscope's metal testing plate.

Chuck Zukowski

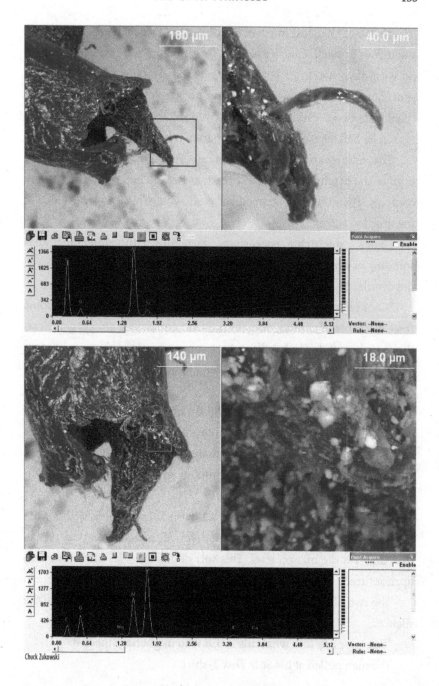

Chuck Zukowski

The object had lost much of its shine since Debbie had pulled it from the dirt at Roswell. Chuck assumed the discoloration had something to do with oxygenation or temperature; he had no idea what the storage procedures had been at the university's archaeology department. The artifact hadn't been catalogued or displayed yet, which had been part of the reason he had been able to get Doleman to release it to him.

The initial scan took about a minute. Chuck could feel the electronic hum of the machine in his lower teeth as he watched the tech work the controls. Then the man stepped back, allowing Chuck to take a look at the imaging screen.

Chuck's microchip background gave him a fundamental understanding of what he was looking at, but he allowed the tech to go through the details.

"Looks like it's predominantly silicon and aluminum. There are some trace elements of carbon, oxygen, and calcium, but we always get those, they're inherent due to handling. I see some manganese in here, but that could be from the dirt at the site. Over and over again, I'm seeing aluminum and silicon."

"Is that a common alloy? Silicon and aluminum?"

"It can be—silicon is often added to aluminum in castings, to reduce melting temperatures and make the material more fluid. But take a closer look at this, man. Manufactured aluminum is usually quite smooth. This is oddly battered and damaged.

"We've got strands sticking out all over. This one here is about ten microns in length. Something violent definitely affected the structure of this, down at the micron level. This sort of damage—it's like it was torn up, fractured."

The two of them stood quietly for a moment, until Chuck broke the silence.

"You have any idea what this is? Or who might have made it?"

The man pulled at his *Star Trek* T-shirt.

"Who? Or what?"

He was grinning, but something in his eyes told Chuck the man was thinking about black helicopters and black ops prison camps again.

"I can tell you one thing, it's definitely not a piece of duct tape."

Chuck wasn't willing to let his imagination go much further than that, but the scan certainly raised questions. Where did this fragment of aluminum and silicon come from? Why did it appear to be damaged? Was it from an impact or something else?

And most important of all: What was this artifact doing in the middle of the New Mexico desert, found under eight to ten centimeters of dirt, dating to approximately 1947, at the proposed Roswell crash debris site?

Maybe it was the yellow lighting, but as he took the artifact off the metal testing plate, he could almost hear the black helicopter rotors himself.

# CHAPTER 21

## NEW EVIDENCE OF UFOS UNCOVERED AT THE INFAMOUS 1947 ROSWELL INCIDENT CRASH SITE

Special Press Conference to Reveal Ground-Breaking Evidence

Thursday, April 30
For Immediate Release.

(ROSWELL, N.M.)—Mystery surrounds the City of Roswell once again as new information surfaces about the discovery of Historic Materials of Uncertain Origin (HMUOs), which will be revealed at a special press conference this Thursday, April 30.

In 2002, an archaeological dig at the Roswell Incident crash site uncovered very small pieces of material that were not indigenous to the Roswell area. Additionally, the landscape itself seemed to have been altered. Only one of the findings has been fully analyzed, the result of which will be divulged at the press conference this week. The ground-breaking research provides more proof that extraterrestrial life visited Earth.

"We're not alone," said former NASA Apollo 14 moon mission astronaut and Roswell native Edgar Mitchell.

—City of Roswell

Chuck leaned back from his computer, bathed in the bluish glow from the screen, and rested his chin on his clasped hands. Apart from the spray of electrified pixels, his office was dark. It had to be well past two in the morning, but Chuck was still wide awake. He hadn't been sleeping well for as long as he could remember—and this had been a particularly trying day.

He undid the top button of his deputy's uniform, letting himself breathe a little easier. He'd been home for at least an hour, now, but he hadn't quite gotten up the energy to change. His leather holster was still hanging from the back of his chair, service revolver still intact. If Tammy had still been awake when he'd gotten home from the day's special detail, she would have been giving him hell for not locking the sidearm in one of the multiple safes he had around the house. She didn't have a problem with Chuck's guns, as long as he followed the house rules.

Then again, even if Tammy had been awake, Chuck doubted she would have bothered him in his office. He wasn't sure when she had officially started avoiding entering the "Batcave," but it couldn't have been long after he'd started to fill in the giant U.S. map still tacked to most of the back wall. The map—along with the numerous data sheets, photographs, and newspaper clippings that were now affixed to nearly every inch of all four office walls, including a handful of cattle mutilation photos taped to the drawn window shades—had changed the atmosphere of the room. The plastic alien toys, robots, sci-fi paraphernalia, and stuffed extraterrestrials were still cluttered on the shelves by the door, but what used to seem like a museum dedicated to one man's quirky hobby had changed into something more severe: Tammy might even have called it "unhinged."

Chuck glanced back from the glowing screen to the map. The colored pinpoints had now spread, like some sort of rainbow-colored viral rash, across much of the Midwest, emanating outward from Colorado Springs. Chuck had still marked only a fraction of his cases—animal mutilations, UFO sightings, other strange anomalies—but already he was beginning to get a sense of the true scale of it all. And this was just his own personal battlefield. He could only imagine what he was going to see when he'd factored in the data from his other colleagues in the field.

Debbie and her MUFON friends probably had maps so professional and detailed, they made his look like the back of a cereal box. But this map showed how far he'd come from his bare-bones beginnings—traipsing through the odd forest or up a nearby mountain to catch sight of unusual lights. His office now looked like a war room, or, as Tammy might say, the frantic pulsing of a "beautiful mind."

Chuck's lips went up at the corners as he shifted his attention back to the computer screen. Sure, to the outside world, to the mainstream, he might look crazy. There was a good reason that he never wore his police uniform when he investigated anomalies. He knew enough to keep that separation between church and state.

Although sometimes the lines got blurred, through no fault of his own. Today had been a perfect example.

When the call had come in, Chuck had known from the start it was going to be a hard detail. He'd never been to the scene of a plane crash before, but he could guess what he was going to see. No matter that it had been a small plane—a Cessna four-seater, with only two passengers, the pilot and a friend. From the moment he'd arrived at the wreckage site, a torn-up field just outside the city limits, he'd been awed by the sheer violence of the impact. Although his job had been roping off the scene with police tape, keeping the press and public away as the emergency teams did their jobs, he had gotten close enough to smell the burning fuel, close enough to see the tangled fiberglass and steel, close enough to see the bodies, or what was left of them.

He didn't know the men who had died in the crash personally, but in his mind he could imagine their final moments. As a cop, he'd seen the aftermath of plenty of car accidents, but there was nothing that could compare to the sheer fury of a high-velocity impact site.

As he'd rolled out the yellow tape, he couldn't help but think back to

Roswell and the strange little fragment, and the cattle mutilations. The way those animals were ripped up seemed like the only thing that came close to the brutality of the plane crash.

Chuck was so caught up thinking about dead cattle and Roswell that he'd almost walked right into the television reporter who was setting up for a long shot of the scene. The man recognized him—but not as a sheriff's deputy.

"Chuck Zukowski? You're a cop?"

Chuck placed the reporter immediately: Andy Koen, from KKTV. Just a few weeks earlier, Koen had shadowed Chuck at the site of one of the cattle mutilations he'd been investigating. As usual, Chuck had been at the ranch without his uniform, and had never let on that he was a reserve sheriff's deputy. The incident had stood out to Chuck—not least because he'd witnessed the moment when the young reporter had shifted from a complete skeptic who believed these mutilations had to be the work of predators or sick pranksters to someone with an open mind. When it happened, Koen had been filming Chuck examining the mutilated cow's mouth, and Chuck had held the jaws open with his gloved hands, asking the reporter to take a look inside for himself. Once Koen had gotten in close, he'd jumped back in shock.

"The tongue has been sliced right out. And it looks like the wound has been cauterized. Like, with some sort of surgical tool."

That hadn't stopped the report that eventually aired on TV from looking like a clip from *The X-Files*, complete with sci-fi music, but at least Chuck had felt he'd made an ally at the station.

"I guess I should have guessed," Koen had said, as he'd continued to prepare for his plane crash spot. "Who else would spend twenty minutes swabbing a dead cow for evidence?"

Chuck had considered the reporter's surprise at seeing him in uniform a testament to the care he had taken to keep his two lives separate. But as he sat in his office later, one glance around him made it clear which life was beginning to dominate the other.

Chuck took a moment to reread the press release that covered most of his computer screen. Although the release had come from the PR department at the Roswell museum, and had primarily been aimed at promoting the upcoming July Fourth festival by using whatever media the "press conference" might draw, Chuck himself was the reason the release had been drafted in the first place.

Chuck had decided to go to the public for help with his Roswell artifact. The decision had not been an easy one; but after going over the findings from the electron microscope scan and talking it through with Debbie, Chuck had realized that the only way he was going to get any deeper understanding of what they had found was to get outside help. He and Debbie couldn't afford to have the fragment analyzed any further on their own. Tammy had put her foot down when Chuck had mentioned how much it might cost to hire lab experts, and Debbie's connections at MUFON had gone nowhere. As Chuck had always maintained, MUFON was all about collecting data; if you wanted to get that data analyzed by real scientists, in real laboratories, you needed to outsource.

Chuck hit a couple of keys on the keyboard, shifting the screen to the information he and Debbie had prepared for the press conference itself:

*My sister and I have found the only artifact from the famous Mac Brazel debris site which resembles the debris Mac, Jesse Marcel and his son had described seeing in 1947. This is very significant and is known to be the only debris in existence which has been acquired scientifically under pristine conditions at the proposed debris site. This artifact could answer one of the following questions:*

1. *Is this artifact from an extraterrestrial craft which crashed at this site in July 1947?*
2. *Is this artifact left over from some type of military presence in this area?*
3. *Why was it so difficult to find this small piece? Could the site*

*where this artifact was found have been cleaned at some point?*
*If so, Why?*

He didn't think he could have gotten any more succinct. The way Tammy had nodded, her cheeks pale, as she'd read it over for him before he'd taken it to Roswell had told him that he hadn't left anything out. It had made Tammy nervous, Chuck's putting himself out there in such a public way, but he'd made up his mind. The whole point of his investigations was to bring this world he'd uncovered into the open. It was time to go public.

Chuck wasn't sure what he expected from the press release and resulting press conference. In the first few days that followed, there was little more than silence. Then, as the news had trickled out through different web forums and a handful of radio shows dedicated to unexplained phenomena, he'd started to get some notice. A few crackpot phone calls, a handful of fan letters, and some friendly notes from the big names in the UFO community ensued.

He'd begun to think that would be the end of his experiment; he'd be left with a strange piece of material from the Roswell dig site, an SEM scan report that hinted at an aluminum silicon alloy that had been damaged, and that would be all. When he'd left for the plane crash detail that morning, he hadn't expected to come home to anything more than his files, his map, and the pinpoints that were gradually spreading across the heart of the country.

To his surprise, he found an email from a scientist—not a crackpot or a fan—willing to take a deeper look at his artifact. Even more surprising, the scientist was from an organization that Chuck had heard about before, in passing. An organization that seemed to share Chuck's interests.

Chuck had immediately gone to work, putting the scientist in touch with the curators at the University of New Mexico, to whom he'd returned the artifact after having it scanned with the SEM.

Clicking past his notes from the press conference, Chuck reopened the last email that the scientist had sent to UNM. Chuck had already borrowed one of the techniques that the military had used to much success in its publicly released files on UFOS, cattle mutilations, and the like: He'd permanently redacted the identity of the scientist, as Chuck intended to eventually put the email on his blog—but the serious manner in which the artifact was being handled was not obscured by any amount of blackening ink:

*To:* ██████████,

 *Sir, my name is* ████████████ *and I am a Program Manager at* ████. *I was asked by Mr. Chuck Zukowski, through Dr. Bill Doleman, to contact you regarding our desire to obtain one of the artifacts maintained at UNM for scientific/laboratory testing. I believe Mr. Zukowski has discussed and identified the specific artifact during previous conversations.*

 *Our testing will be conducted to determine if there is any significant scientific value of the artifact, as we are focused on advanced aerospace technologies.*

 *The lab/company that will be conducting the initial testing is* ████████ *in* ████████. *The initial testing will be XRF non-destructive analysis. Further testing requirements will be determined after analysis of the XRF results.*

 *If there are other matters in which I can be of assistance, please do not hesitate to ask. Of note, I will be out of the office until Monday, July 26.*

 *We look forward to acquiring the artifact for analysis.*

*Very Sincerely,*

████████████

*Program Manager*
*Bigelow Aerospace Advanced Space Studies*

The wheels were now in motion; Chuck had already gotten confirmation from Doleman that the artifact would soon be on its way to the experts at Bigelow Aerospace Advanced Space Studies.*

Bigelow was familiar to Chuck; he'd read plenty of articles about the NIDS and especially its continuing study of Skinwalker Ranch in Utah. Chuck had frequently come across reports from Skinwalker, and he'd read everything that the scientists from NIDS had publicly written about the anomalies that had occurred on the Ute Indian land. Chuck also knew the rumors that swirled through the UFO community whenever Bigelow's name was mentioned—the purported CIA ties, the possibility that Bigelow was more involved with extraterrestrial phenomena than he'd ever admit.

And Chuck had even seen Bigelow himself in person; they'd crossed paths at a UFO conference in California, where Bigelow had spoken in front of a large audience about NIDS and the importance of putting real science behind UFO studies. Chuck had been impressed by the man's determination, and he and Bigelow shared a belief that the only way to get the world to look at these anomalies seriously was to offer real science instead of stories, math instead of myth.

But as familiar as Chuck was with Bigelow and the NIDS, he'd never heard of Bigelow Aerospace Advanced Space Studies. A real estate mogul obsessed with UFOs was intriguing enough; a billionaire who had somehow turned an interest in UFOs into an aerospace company seemed like something out of a James Bond movie. Add to these facts that Bigelow owned Skinwalker Ranch and had closed it to the public, and he had

---

* BAASS—Bigelow Aerospace Advanced Space Studies—is considered a distinct entity from Bigelow Aerospace, which is Robert Bigelow's space technology company currently developing expandable space station modules. BAASS has described itself as "a research organization that focuses on the identification, evaluation, and acquisition of novel and emerging future technologies worldwide as they specifically relate to spacecraft." References to Bigelow Aerospace and BAASS are not meant to be interchangeable, and any references regarding Bigelow as related to UFO studies refer to BAASS.

linked UFO sightings to a black ops air force program to develop electrokinetic blimps, and you had the makings of a frightening conspiracy
story.

For the moment, Chuck intended to keep the conspiracy thoughts at
bay. For whatever reasons, a Bigelow scientist wanted to study the artifact
Chuck had found at Roswell. Bigelow had the resources, and apparently
the necessary laboratory equipment, to conduct such a study; maybe
Chuck had found the perfect ally to further this particular investigation.

He didn't need to trust Bigelow to let his people take a look, any more
than he needed to trust MUFON to let his sister partner with him on his
adventures.

As he finally turned off the computer screen and stood up from his
desk, he cast one last look at the U.S. map—his gaze gravitating from the
bunched-up red pushpins representing cattle mutilations spread across
Colorado, Utah, and Nevada to the green points around Roswell, linking
upward toward Washington State and Kenneth Arnold's original flying
saucers.

A few minutes passed in silence before he turned back to his bedroom,
ready to chase the last few hours of sleep before he needed to head back to
police headquarters to file his report on the day's unpleasant detail.

He wasn't sure what made him detour to the shaded window on his
way out of the office, or what pushed him to pull aside one of the photographs pinned to the shade just enough for him to peer between the thick
material and through the darkened pane of glass.

It took him a moment to find the parked SUV, two tires resting
against the curb directly across the street from his house. As he watched,
the SUV's headlights blinked on, and the car slowly rolled forward. Only
when it reached the curb by his neighbor's front lawn did the SUV begin
to accelerate. A few seconds later, it was gone.

# CHAPTER 22

## NORTH LAS VEGAS, NEVADA, AUGUST 2008

Jeff Foust

*The fastest way to make a small fortune in the aerospace industry is to start with a large one.*

The thought wasn't original; in fact, Robert Bigelow had borrowed it from his sometime colleague, sometime competitor in the private, commercial space race, Elon Musk, but at the moment it seemed particularly apropos. Standing in the center of the command center of Bigelow Aerospace Mission Control—surrounded by millions of dollars in equipment, caught in the glow of multiple giant screens hanging from the ceiling, above row after row of oblong workstations, staffed by dozens of the top aerospace engineers money could drag to his secure, somewhat fortresslike fifty-acre compound in a residential/commercial suburb ten miles north of the Las Vegas Strip— Bigelow couldn't help but think about hard numbers. At his heart, Bigelow was a businessman, and his mind naturally gravitated to dollars spent and dollars to be spent—even when the business at hand had very little to do with earthly balance sheets, cost/earning calculations, or profits.

Unlike Musk or the handful of other daring entrepreneurs who had turned their attention to the privatization of space, Bigelow wasn't actually in it for the money. Although he envisioned a future that included a vast return on investments in the industry, he hadn't pledged half his entire fortune—*five hundred million dollars*—to building his own private NASA, one thirty-dollar taxi ride from the Bellagio's famous fountains, to make money. And though Bigelow Aerospace had all the accoutrements of a real corporate endeavor—top-flight engineers, more than 120 employees including former astronauts, department heads from the real NASA, an accounting team, a human resources department, at least one Washington legal division, and a two-building Vegas complex protected by razor wire and armed guards—the endeavor was much more than a simple offshoot of the real estate empire that had made him a billionaire.

Bigelow let his terrestrial thoughts of dollar signs drift away as he watched the images shifting across the many television screens; interior and exterior shots of one of the two beautiful, oblong monuments to a dream on its way to being realized, floating through the blackness of a deep and perfect orbit. *Genesis II*, Bigelow's brainchild, was depicted spinning along in space in real time at 17,000 mph, 350 miles up—a full 75 miles higher than the International Space Station. And though the object might have been confused with some sort of communications satellite, the flotsam of some television or radio conglomerate making use of 1960s-era technology to allow Hollywood producers to beam idiotic sitcoms and dumbed-down news programs to every suburban corner of the globe, the Bigelow craft was something much more significant. At the moment, *Genesis* represented a technology in its infancy; technology that Bigelow believed would one day be epochal.

The steps that had led Bigelow from Budget Suites to Bigelow Aerospace, and *Genesis*—by way of the NIDS, it could be said—had been a mixture of accident and applied imagination. Although space had always been his goal—for what he assumed to be very different reasons from the ones that possessed men like Elon Musk and those who ran his competitors in the industry—he had at first approached his dream like the real estate mogul he was. The ideas he'd first advanced, dutifully documented by awed and amused local and national journalists, had been met by much skepticism: hotels in space, a resort on the Moon, even an orbital cruise liner. He'd dreamed up numerous ways to take his real estate skills beyond Earth's atmosphere. But when he'd stumbled on an article in *Air & Space/Smithsonian* magazine, about a defunct NASA project called TransHab, he'd locked into an idea worth his five-hundred-million-dollar pledge.

Although his attention remained pinned to the screens showing the *Genesis* module arcing through its orbit, his mind wandered to the airport-hangar-sized manufacturing hall where his TransHab project had grown from a NASA idea to two full-fledged, working prototypes for Transit Habitat.

Isaac Brekken/*The New York Times*/Redux

Bigelow had been captivated by the idea of inflatable habitats, made of puncture-proof, radiation-resistant, stronger-than-steel space-age materials. The genius of the modules was in their design; deflated, they were small enough to be launched as payload in a variety of rockets, taking up less space than any modern satellite. Once in orbit, they could be inflated into habitats large enough to provide living and working space for multiple astronauts. *Genesis I* and *II*, designed as the first test modules, encompassed four floors and were over 14 feet by 8 feet in size, with an interior around 406 cubic feet. But at launch, they could shrink to a diameter of 5 feet—smaller than any capsule that had ever held an astronaut.

The *Genesis* models were only the beginning, the proof of concept. Originally, NASA's idea for the TransHab had involved a Mars mission that had been too expensive to ever come to fruition: to attach multiple TransHab units together to create a livable structure on Mars. Bigelow's design team had extended this vision; his idea was first to attach modules to the International Space Station, to replace the already existing crew Habitation Module of the International Space Station, and eventually to plant his own space station in orbit, then after that—on the Moon.

From the very beginning, Bigelow had believed that the TransHab could be the backbone of the private space industry. If NASA didn't have the will—or the dollars—to move forward with the space race, Bigelow—along with Musk, and many others—felt that it was up to the private sector to do it.

Although NASA held the patents on the device, Bigelow had moved quickly to take over the project. Three years of negotiation and he was able to buy the rights to the idea, at which point he'd discovered that the technology and materials necessary to make the TransHab work were nowhere near as developed as advertised. So he'd put together a team of top engineers, many culled from NASA's ranks, to build the damn thing.

Once the units were built, the problem became how to get the whole thing into space. There simply weren't many options. Musk's first Space X launch of a viable earth-to-orbit rocket was still a year away at the time *Genesis I* was ready, and NASA had apparently given up on putting large objects—let alone ones that could hold astronauts—into space.

While searching out international partners for his endeavor, he'd gotten a bizarre offer from a joint Russian-Ukrainian team from the ISC Kosmotras Space and Missile Complex near Yasny, Russia. Essentially, the Russians suggested that they could remove the warhead from a nuclear missile and attach Bigelow's payload to a former ICBM.

The nuclear missile was already at the ready, in a silo; all that needed to be changed was the target. Instead of some city in the United States, the Russians could aim their missile into orbit, and Bigelow's TransHab would be on its way. It seemed strangely fitting: As a kid, Bigelow had watched mushroom clouds; that same technology would now allow him to place the first piece of livable, private property into space.

Partnering with a nuclear missile base had its own peculiar set of obstacles. Since Bigelow Aerospace was an American company, the U.S. Defense Department demanded that its agents be present at every meeting with the Russian technical teams. In an odd twist, Bigelow's company had to pay for the agents who were sent to monitor him and his partners. One engineer observing the process had joked that at least in the Cold War with the Russians, the KGB had spied on them for free.

Aside from the missile itself, most of the technical specs of the former Soviet nuclear base seemed primitive compared to NASA's; spotty Internet access, minimal hot water and heat, barracks made for a military used to spartan conditions, not Texan and Nevadan engineers. But the launch ended up a success, and once in orbit, the TransHab operated exactly as the engineers had predicted. Fully inflated, it could have kept four astronauts comfortable and healthy for years. Of course, since it had been merely the first test of the technology, instead of live astronauts, *Genesis* had been filled with playing cards, toy cars, a Superman action figure, and the very first Sponge Bob in space. *Genesis II*, sent up a year later, was a successful second proof of concept—and Bigelow Aerospace had also proven itself to be a force at the forefront of the privatization of space.

To Bigelow himself, the success of the TransHab was only the beginning. He'd given up on his plans of a space hotel or an orbital cruise ship, but his focus on the Moon had not waned. NASA's obsession with putting men on Mars or on asteroids—something that would take decades, at best, to accomplish—was shortsighted. The Moon, to Bigelow, was real estate that made sense: technologically habitable, full of potential resources, and a good first step toward a permanent space residency. Putting a permanent base in space had always been Bigelow's aim.

Watching the TransHab spin across the screens in his private mission control, he was amazed at how far he'd come in such a relatively short time, without ever losing sight of his original goals. He'd closed down the NIDS, but he'd rolled what he'd been trying to accomplish with these scientific teams into Bigelow Aerospace. Now he had a two-pronged strategy: use the TransHab to reach space from Earth, while engaging the aerospace company's labs and resources to continue the research into anomalies that might represent space life coming to Earth.

Even with its successes, the aerospace company hadn't quieted the Internet chatter or conspiracy theories; now more than ever, Bigelow was described as "reclusive" and "mysterious"—though in his mind, he couldn't have been clearer about his intentions. He wasn't hiding anything, giving interviews such as the one he'd done with *Air & Space/Smithsonian* magazine just a few months earlier, in which he'd told a journalist that "he'd often accompanied NIDS teams, flying the team on his private jet," and that of the existence of UFOs "I have no doubt."

Hell, the Bigelow Aerospace logo even had an alien front and center.

Hotel mogul Robert Bigelow sits in an office at Bigelow Aerospace headquarters outside Las Vegas, where he hopes to build the world's first orbital hotel, the CSS Skywalker.

Bigelow Aerospace headquarters outside Las Vegas.

Security guard patrolling past barbed-wire fence at Bigelow Aerospace.

But Bigelow's admissions only seemed to feed the theories. And the truth was, now that he was involved in the space race, he did have deals and ties with the U.S. government. He not only had contacts with the Defense Department over his use of a Soviet nuclear base for his launch as well as NASA because of the TransHab, but he'd also connected with the FAA over the UFO issue itself.

Because no known government agencies were currently looking into the phenomenon, Bigelow had offered his own services—and the FAA had responded, eager to offer pilots some sort of reporting mechanism that wouldn't reek of career suicide. Outsourcing pilot reports of strange anomalies made sense to the pilots as well, as they knew the skepticism they would face from reporting UFOs up the official chain of command. Ironic, considering pilots were the first people to bring the UFO phenomenon to the modern public.

Still, it was gratifying to see the new, official guidelines put into words, right in the FAA manuals:

> **4-7-4. UNIDENTIFIED FLYING OBJECT (UFO) REPORTS**
>
> **a.** Persons wanting to report UFO/unexplained phenomena activity should contact a UFO/ unexplained phenomena reporting data collection center, such as Bigelow Aerospace Advanced Space Studies (BAASS) (voice: 1-877-979-7444 or e-mail: Reporting@baass.org), the National UFO Reporting Center, etc.
>
> **b.** If concern is expressed that life or property might be endangered, report the activity to the local law enforcement department.

**1. PARAGRAPH NUMBER AND TITLE:** 1-2-5. ABBREVIATIONS, and 4-7-4. UNIDENTIFIED FLYING OBJECT (UFO) REPORTS

**2. BACKGROUND:** Bigelow Aerospace Advanced Space Studies (BAASS) is a new organization that is devoted to exploration of extremely advanced aerospace technology, including the so-called unidentified aerial phenomena (UAP) or unidentified flying object (UFO) topics. In 2001, another of Mr. Bigelow's organizations, the National Institute for Discovery Sciences (NIDS), succeeded in becoming the "go-to" organization for the reporting by pilots and air traffic

## control of UFOs in the United States.

U.S. Department of Transportation, Federal Aviation Administration (FAA), Air Traffic Organization P

What would conspiracy theorists and the general public think if they realized that, right in the FAA handbook, there was a section on what a pilot was supposed to do when he encountered a UFO? Even more astonishing, the pilot was ordered to report the sighting, not to a government agency, but to Bigelow Aerospace Advanced Space Studies, a sister company to Bigelow Aerospace, a private space company, whose eventual goal was to build an inflatable space station on the Moon.

Bigelow was open about his beliefs, but he wasn't a fool, and he understood the need to keep some things secret. Speaking to *Air & Space*, he'd voiced his concerns about what might happen when UFOs were eventually proven to be real: "Will people go to the gun store? Buy up everything? Hide in their houses? Will deliveries get made, or will people go to work?"

Maybe the shadows were where his work belonged. He didn't need the press, the government, or the public. He had plenty of resources to conduct his research, while building toward his own expansion into space. He had access to reports from varied sources and government agencies, as well as his still-operating NIDS report hotline, which he'd left functioning even after he'd shut down the center. He'd also been looking into finding some way to partner with the national network of UFO enthusiasts, MUFON, although he had his reservations about MUFON, which he considered a chaotic gathering dominated by believers, rather than scientists. Nonetheless, he believed that with the right organizational changes, MUFON might be able to conduct quality investigations, as the NIDS had done. At worst, MUFON was another avenue to gather reports, which his own scientists could study.

Lowering himself into a high-backed chair at a kidney-shaped console beneath the glowing television screens at Bigelow Aerospace, Bigelow listened to the chatter of his engineers, discussing altitudes, temperatures, and pressure gauges. When he was a kid, it would have sounded like so much science fiction; now it was simply science. And this compound, which wouldn't have been out of place in a pulp comic of his youth, was a working mission control at the forefront of the space race. At the same time, Bigelow saw it as the de facto mission control of an even more significant calling.

The farther he moved into space, the more convinced he had become that his childhood beliefs could be proven by science. He hadn't yet found the irrefutable evidence, but he believed he would.

He was reminded of a recent meeting he'd had with believers in the industry, including intelligence officers, a former astronaut, and former air force officials. Off the record, the conversation had quickly shifted from the TransHab to UFOs. Upper-echelon officials from the military, intelligence, and aerospace worlds had seen enough in their careers to believe, and they were looking to Bigelow to one day provide the concrete evidence.

As one of the few people on Earth with a real foothold in space, Bigelow believed that evidence was closer than ever before: one small step, one giant leap.

*Night view of Las Vegas Strip as seen through barbed-wire fence at Bigelow Aerospace.*

# CHAPTER 23

The parallel bands of razor wire shimmered like plucked guitar strings, electrifying the overheated air rising from the expanse of asphalt that separated the outskirts of the fortified compound of Bigelow Aerospace from the two perpendicular industrial buildings. Chuck estimated the distance at more than a quarter mile, but enhanced by the sophisticated glass prism of his pair of high-powered, military-grade binoculars, it felt much closer. All he had to do was climb off the hood of his jeep, exit the second-floor parking garage where he'd set up his morning stakeout, and jog over to the weakest section of the wire fence—right up at the edge of the compound's employee parking area, where one of the fence posts seemed to be nearly rusted through, after an early spring rainstorm that had blown through a week earlier. A bit of grounding tape, a few snips with the metal shears Chuck kept in his equipment pack in the trunk of his jeep, and he'd be on his way inside. On his way to the answers that had been evading him for a frustrating eight months.

Of course, he knew better than to do this. Shifting his binoculars to the right, he could easily make out the security booth by the gated front driveway of the complex. Although the guards weren't visible, he'd seen them before, up close and in person, young men who wouldn't have cared less about his sheriff's department ID, even if he'd carried it with him. These private guards, strapped with 9 mm handguns, carried clipboards with lists of names of people they could admit to the premises, which would never include a UFO hunter from Colorado Springs.

Even if he'd cut his way through the wire and sneaked inside the compound, he guessed he'd have found himself up against armed guards and sophisticated security systems, from doors with electronic combination locks to hallways lined with infrared, motion-detecting cameras. And if he somehow got past the guns and the electronics—what then? Would he sneak from lab to lab, searching through files that were nearly a year old, trying to solve a riddle embedded in email chains, ignored phone calls, and deafening silence? Was this even the right place? Wasn't BAASS a distinct entity from Bigelow Aerospace? Bigelow Aerospace was a top-flight space technology company. Not a lab that studied objects that might have come from UFOs."

Chuck lowered the binoculars, letting his chin rest against the cold metal of the car. Hell, he wasn't even sure what he was doing there, what had compelled him to make the twelve-hour drive from Colorado Springs. Maybe the little voice in his head was right. Maybe he'd crossed that fine line between healthy paranoia and true crazy a few hundred miles ago. But after so many months of being ignored—of so much goddamn silence—he'd *had* to do something.

The most frustrating part of the situation was that at the beginning, there had been so much promise. After the scientists at BAASS had contacted Chuck, he'd gotten the curators at UNM to carve off a small fragment from the Roswell artifact, seal it into an airtight container, and ship it off to Bigelow's labs. Chuck had gone back to his life; days that mixed deputy duties and microchip work, nights spent trawling through newspapers and MUFON reports for nearby UFO sightings or fresh cattle mutilations. Whenever something good came up, he was back in the RV, sometimes with Tammy and the kids, sometimes with Debbie, sometimes on his own, going up into the mountains with his night-vision goggles and his cameras or out onto the ranches, collecting samples, calming ranchers.

In the back of his mind, though, he never stopped wondering about that piece of metallic material that Debbie had pulled out of the Roswell dirt. And no matter how many months went by, he checked his email by the hour. He realized that he was giving Tammy even more evidence that he was sliding down that slope, from hobby to passion to obsession. She'd almost convinced him that his OCD-level vigilance was a waste of time, that a big, billion-dollar company had no time for or interest in a small-town UFO nut like Chuck, when he'd opened up his email, one Sunday afternoon, and found the long-awaited response sitting in his inbox:

*From: BAAS* ▉▉▉▉▉▉▉▉▉▉
*Sent:* ▉▉▉▉▉▉▉▉▉▉
*To: 'Zukowski'*
*Subject: RE: Roswell Artifact Update?*

*Here is the preliminary study, there is currently a discussion on whether to continue with isotope analysis. I will let you know the outcome.*

————————————————

*Analysis of Roswell Crash Site Samples*

*Our x-ray fluorescence (XRF) system consists of an X-123SDD Silicon Drift Detector and a 40 kV Mini-X x-ray tube made by the AMPTEK Corporation. The detector has an energy resolution of 136 eV FWHM at 5.9 keV. This system permits non-destructive identification and semi-quantitative analysis of all elements heavier than Si in a wide variety of samples including liquids, powders, and solids.*

*We typically perform the analysis in air, meaning there will be a significant peak from argon in all of our spectra.*

*The material provided is a dark gray polymer that contains small amounts of several elements that are commonly used as colorants (iron, zinc, calcium, titanium). We were not able to identify any mass-produced polymer that matches this sample, but the number of products to compare to is immense. The sample does not contain any elements that wouldn't be expected in a standard polymer.*

For Chuck, it was a mixed result, but exciting nonetheless. Although Bigelow's scientists found some elements "commonly used as colorants," to Chuck the most significant description of their lab analysis was: "We were not able to identify any mass-produced polymer that matches this sample."

To Chuck, that meant that the fragment was not a piece of duct tape—or any other easily identifiable material. Reading through the analysis again and again, Chuck wondered why the lab hadn't found the high levels of aluminum and silicon he had seen in the electron microscope report. To his surprise, the Bigelow scientist was instantly available, and happy to answer the question.

*From: BAAS* ▓▓▓▓▓▓▓▓▓
*Sent:* ▓▓▓▓▓▓▓▓▓▓▓▓
*To: 'Zukowski'*
*Subject: RE: Roswell Artifact Update?*

*Chuck, the lab replied as follows:*
*"As stated in the description of our XRF system, we are capable of reliable analysis of only those elements heavier than Si because we operate in air and use a Mylar window. Unfortunately, aluminum is at the ragged edge of our detection limit. Under favorable conditions (such as with a large specimen that is a majority aluminum, i.e., an aluminum alloy like 6061), we are able to see a small peak to indicate*

*the presence of the element. With the sample tested, not only the size but the relatively small quantity of aluminum, we would be unable to detect its presence."*

By Chuck's reading, the lab couldn't account for aluminum or silicon, but their analysis had clearly shown that, whatever the material was that Chuck and Debbie had found at Roswell, it wasn't something the scientists had seen before. They couldn't identify any polymer that matched the sample; that didn't mean it was extraterrestrial in origin, but it wasn't something that could easily be explained away. The scientists further stated that they were engaging in discussions to determine what other tests they could run to try to identify the polymer and told Chuck they'd get back to him.

Chuck had excitedly shown Tammy the emails, and had been surprised when she shrugged at them. To her, they were inconclusive. They couldn't identify the material; that was all the email stated. Chuck had countered with more facts: The fragment had been found lying in 1947-era dirt, and matched the description of the debris that had been discovered at the time of the Roswell crash, but Tammy considered all of that circumstantial. She might as well have been a lawyer, tearing down his case piece by piece.

In spite of Tammy's skepticism, Chuck felt certain that, as Bigelow's lab looked closer into the fragment, using more sophisticated equipment, they would find something concrete, undeniable. So he had begun the painful wait again, checking his email hour after hour, day after day.

And—nothing. Total silence. No matter how many emails he sent to the scientists, he did not receive a response. A few months later, he began calling the company directly, trying to get to the scientist who'd written the emails, then searching out anyone in the company directory who might have information about the labs dedicated to unknown materials research. Again, nothing. He was shuttled to various voice mails, and never received any response.

His frustration grew. Either Tammy was right—the inconclusive lab results had left Bigelow uninterested in pursuing more lab work—or they were ignoring Chuck for another reason. His mind imagined possibilities: Could they have found something important and decided that it was too big to involve some UFO hunter in Colorado? Were they keeping their lab results private? Did they have evidence of alien technology that they had their own use for?

He was treading a dangerous path, letting his thoughts go into the shadows, but the longer he went without receiving a response, the more the conspiracy theorists seemed to make sense. What was Bigelow truly up to? What sort of materials was the company making for inflatable habitats that could survive in the harsh environment of space? And where were they getting such technology?

Chuck wasn't entirely sure what had finally spurred him to pack his equipment into the jeep and head out onto the road. But he was certain that Tammy wouldn't have approved.

There was a big difference between actively lying to your wife and simply avoiding a conversation. Tammy had already left for work when he'd decided to take the exploratory trip. Even though he knew he was breaking a cardinal rule—she was supposed to know where he was whenever he went on one of his adventures—he was pretty sure how that phone call would have gone. She'd have called him crazy and paranoid for thinking a major aerospace company was hiding evidence of alien technology, and that he could just show up and demand answers from a reclusive billionaire.

She would have been right on the second point: Showing up and demanding answers had gotten him nowhere. He now found himself leaning against the hood of his car a quarter mile away, with a pair of binoculars.

He shook his head, then raised the binoculars again, guiding the powerful lenses down the long, shimmering strands of wire. When he reached the far corner of the compound, he shifted the binoculars toward the main building itself—pausing on that strange logo etched into the high left corner of the outer wall. Right there, for the entire world to see— an alien drawn right onto the side of the building. If Bigelow truly did have something to hide, it wasn't his interest in extraterrestrials. Bigelow seemed to be making it quite clear that his company was engaged in the same hunt as Chuck himself, the same hobby that had turned into an obsession.

The question was, had they found something real? *Something worth covering up?*

Chuck's thoughts were interrupted by a dull vibration in his shirt pocket. He retrieved his phone within, shifting his gaze from the alien embedded in the concrete wall.

"I've got good news for you," Debbie's voice echoed in his ear, amplified by the parking garage. "You've been approved."

It took Chuck a moment to understand what his sister was talking about. "You're kidding."

"I'm not kidding, but I am really jealous. First Star Team mission and it's my freaky little brother. I guess the moral of the story is, expertise trumps personality. And looks. And hygiene—"

Chuck cut her off with a flick of his finger and lowered the binoculars. Her news didn't make the frustration, anger, and disappointment go away, but the adrenaline was rising through his system. One door seemed to have closed, but another had just been flung open. The strange thing was, the hinges of both doors were related, by the same bizarre logo.

# CHAPTER 24

## DURAN RANCH, WESTON, COLORADO,
## MARCH 15, 2009

37.1328° N, 104.8475° W

One boot in the stream, down to the ankle in the cold, muddy water, cast concentric ripples out behind Chuck like the blast waves of a liquid supernova. The other boot, sunk into the reddish mud at the edge of the streambed, was braced at the heel against an overturned stone. By all reason, by all objective goddamn reason, that stone should have been drenched red in blood, so close was it to the cow's carcass. Leaning forward at the knees, his hands clenched against the hilt of the power saw, Chuck steadied the blade over the excise site, a spot beneath where the udders should have been—had they not already been removed—the spot where the poor animal's reproductive organs had also already been carved out in a perfect oval.

"Ready?" Chuck asked, as he prepared to get his sample.

He glanced over his gauze surgical mask toward the ponytailed man on the other side of the cow, Joe Fex, his volunteer assistant on the mission, the part Native American he'd met years earlier at a UFO gathering. An intuitive outdoorsman, part Blackfoot and Cree, with ancestors hailing from present-day Montana, Fex was an excellent investigator in his own right. His Native American background gave him a unique understanding of the natural—and unnatural—twists that such an investigation could involve.

"There won't be any blood," Chuck continued. "But it's still going to be tough, getting through the muscle and into the bone."

Joe blinked above his own gauze mask, as he bent over at the waist beneath his gray-green working overalls, his gloved hands reaching down to help hold the animal steady beneath the saw.

"Gets more glamorous by the moment, Chuck."

"Well, what the hell were you expecting? Tuxedos and caviar?"

"I don't know," Joe responded, his voice partially muffled by the gauze of his mask. "Silver jumpsuits? Or maybe one of those black helicopters we keep hearing about?"

"We're not superheroes or secret agents. And this isn't *Mission Impossible*."

"Nevertheless," Joe said.

Chuck let the word hang in the fetid air between them as he focused his attention on the circular wound beneath the animal's missing udder. Chuck wasn't going to admit it to Joe, but he had expected more as well.

When Debbie had called him with the news, he had almost been able to hear the first bars of the *Mission Impossible* theme song. Debbie's revelation—that the cattle mutilation file Chuck had submitted to the MUFON directors had been chosen as the basis for the first official Star Team investigation—had filled him with pride and surprise. Even though he'd rejoined MUFON at Debbie's prodding, he still considered himself an outsider, and he hadn't expected that one of his cattle mutilation reports would catch the attention of an organization predominantly interested in UFOs. The Star Team program wasn't simply a MUFON directive. It represented the first real cooperation of MUFON, a national organization of amateur UFO hunters, and a major, if mysterious, corporate entity with possible government ties: *Bigelow Aerospace Advanced Space Studies.*

As Debbie had explained it, the relationship between MUFON and BAASS had been initiated after a late 2008 meeting between the heads of MUFON, James Carrion, Jan Harzan, Chuck Modlin, and John Schuessler, and Robert Bigelow, whose goal had been to find some method to establish cooperation between the two organizations. Bigelow's interest in UFOs was well known; his company was gathering UFO data and analyzing evidence in its labs. Bigelow was also putting its own well-funded investigators into the field—placing scientists at sites like Skinwalker Ranch and sending agents to look for more of those Big Black Deltas they believed were secret experimental air force blimps.

At the 2008 meeting, a deal was struck. BAASS would fund MUFON-organized, rapid-response teams that could dive into "high-value UFO cases" within twenty-four hours of a reported sighting. They would be called Star Teams. The Star Teams would represent the cream of the MUFON crop—the most experienced investigators doing the most groundbreaking work. Bigelow would fund only investigations that involved major "physical trace" UFO events, category 2 or 3 in the MUFON lexicon. More than fifty of Bigelow's own scientists would assist as consultants, providing lab analysis of whatever was found in the field. On the surface, it was a spectacular development: a major aeronautics company funding a UFO response team through the MUFON organization.

Chuck had his reservations about the arrangement; his own experience with Bigelow and his Roswell fragment told him that the company was decidedly less than transparent with its findings. Through the Star Team program, Bigelow would have access to MUFON reports and field work, and could take whatever evidence was found and do whatever the hell it wanted with it; if Bigelow actually found an alien connection, would MUFON, or the general public, ever know?

But still, being chosen for the first Star Team investigation was a thrill and an honor. After Debbie's call, and a conversation with MUFON headquarters, Chuck had immediately driven back to Colorado, along the way assembling his team and putting together the equipment he would need. Then he'd contacted the rancher, Mike Duran, and headed toward Weston, near Trinidad, a stretch of desert ranch land 150 miles from Colorado Springs.

Chuck had first been clued in to the Duran mutilation entirely by accident. He'd been on his couch in his house, watching the local evening news. A brief report on the incident had included an aerial view of the mutilation site. What he'd seen in that brief few-second shot had immediately compelled him to call the KOAA television reporter as well as the related county sheriff's office requesting more information on the case. He'd reached the deputy in charge of the investigation and gotten as much information as he could on what was now Criminal Case #09-00155, the suspicious death and mutilation of a six-hundred-dollar, twenty-eight-year-old cow. According to the case report, the animal had been found on its left side near the bank of the Purgatoire River, its reproductive organs and udder removed via circular cuts, with no blood or signs of physical trauma. The wounds seemed cauterized, and the closest cow prints ended four feet away from the carcass. No noticeable vehicle tire prints, no signs of scavengers. The deputy in charge considered the case open and unusual.

Chuck agreed, though to him, it wasn't the mutilation itself that seemed unusual; he had a filing cabinet filled with similar mutilations. It was the area around the mutilation that he had first seen on the TV report that had immediately caused him to file the report with MUFON and to ask that the investigation be considered for Star Team status.

MUFON—and Bigelow—had apparently agreed with his assessment, and Debbie had called to give him the go-ahead. But after he'd returned from north Las Vegas and called the rancher, put together his resources, called Joe in, and was halfway to the site, Debbie called again to say that

MUFON and Bigelow had suddenly, inexplicably, changed their minds. Chuck's euphoria at being the first Star Team investigator was short-lived.

Star Team status had been pulled even before Chuck had taken his first sample at the Duran ranch. According to Debbie, for whatever reason, Bigelow had informed MUFON it was not going to sanction the case as an official Star Team investigation, that in general, unless an animal mutilation had direct connection with a UFO, it was not going to be funded by the aerospace company.

Chuck felt as if the rug had been pulled out from under him, but since everything was already in motion, he'd decided to continue the investigation on his own. Without Bigelow, MUFON didn't have the resources to run any analysis on any evidence he might find, so it was going to be all out of Chuck's pocket, and he'd have to find his own means to conduct whatever research made sense.

His boot sank deeper into the mud of the streambed as he moved the edge of the saw blade closer to the animal's skin. Joe flinched, though his grip didn't loosen on the cow's haunches. Keeping the target steady, Joe was taking the mission seriously. Although Chuck hadn't gone into detail about what it meant that the investigation had at least momentarily been of Star Team status, he'd communicated the gravity of the mutilation site. This wasn't *Mission Impossible*, but there was no doubt that something horrible and mysterious had occurred at this streambed, and that the rancher, out looking for his missing cow, had stumbled on a scene worthy of at least one black helicopter.

The saw touched meat, and Chuck carefully worked around the strange circular incision, coring out what he hoped to be enough of a bio sample for the analysis he had planned for later in the day. He'd never gotten a sample this fresh before. This was his first rapid-response case, even without the Star Team designation, but even so, it wasn't the mutilated cow itself that most excited him about the moment—it was a ground anomaly at the Duran site, which he had first seen on that aerial TV report.

Chuck Zukowski

After he removed the bio sample and bagged it in one of his police evidence containers, he shifted his attention away from the carcass, up toward the fields that spread down to the streambed. He shielded his eyes from the sun for a clear look at the ground anomaly.

Chuck Zukowski

Even from ground level, the dark scar in the distant field was clearly visible. In a moment, Chuck and his big assistant would trek over to the spot for soil samples. Chuck had no idea what he was going to do with them. After his experience with the Roswell fragment, sending them to Bigelow was out of the question, but he didn't really care. This was the first cattle mutilation he'd been associated with that included such a ground anomaly. Maybe Bigelow didn't see evidence here of a strong enough connection to UFOs to call this a Star Team mission, but to Chuck, it was definitely worth digging into. This was something he hadn't seen before and here, boots in red mud, with a mutilated cow carcass at his feet, he felt deep in his own element. He didn't need Bigelow's money or MUFON's blessing to tell him he was exactly where he was meant to be.

He smiled beneath his gauze mask as he headed toward that scarred soil in the nearby field.

# CHAPTER 25

## COLORADO SPRINGS,
## APRIL 5, 2009

"Something stinks in here," said Tammy.

Chuck had the car radio up high enough to make the dashboard tremble, some country song he couldn't identify. His eyes were on the highway, sun going down in the distance, asphalt snaking out ahead of them between strips of green, but his mind was somewhere else, in a lab decked out in chrome, glass, and porcelain, with young men and women in blue scrubs and white coats gathered around a metal autopsy table.

"Really, Chuck. I don't care if you hit the drive-thru on your way to pick me up. But you've got to throw out your trash afterward. It smells like the alley behind a butcher's shop in here."

The desiccated organs—the ones that were still where they were supposed to be—were white and crumbling. Scalpels and forceps, and a frightening tool called a rib-spreader, were held aloft by gloved hands. And then the wide eyes above the surgical masks, expressions that told him everything he needed to know.

"Chuck," Tammy repeated.

"Open your window," he said. "Let the breeze in."

"My window is open."

Chuck looked over and saw that Tammy did indeed have the passenger window open; she was leaning her head out over the highway, as far as the seat-belt would allow. Her hair floated around her like a demented halo. She was still in the suit she'd worn to work that morning at the delivery station of the packing plant, a conservative gray number with too many buttons, closed up tight around her neck. Usually, she drove herself home, or carpooled with one of the other women who worked in packaging at the multinational. But her car had broken down in the parking lot after lunch, and she couldn't arrange a better option. When she'd called Chuck that afternoon, he hadn't dared make up an excuse for why he couldn't give her a lift.

And the truth was completely out of the question.

"I don't see any wrappers, though," she said, holding her nose as she pulled her head back into the truck, glancing around the floor beneath her feet. "Why don't I see any wrappers?"

Chuck shifted his attention back to the road. A few cars were ahead of him, a VW bug in his lane and a pair of Japanese makes in the two lanes on either side. Then he glanced in the rearview mirror, doing his best not to catch Tammy's eyes.

"Chuck."

A flatbed truck directly behind him, but far enough back that he couldn't see what sort of load it was carrying. Next to that, a green Kia, two teenagers in the front seat.

"Chuck."

He looked at her and watched the color creep out of her cheeks.

"Is there a dead cow in the back of this truck?"

Chuck paused for as long as he dared.

"It's not the whole cow."

"Chuck!"

It was true, it wasn't the whole cow, just the hind legs and most of the head. There hadn't been enough of the torso left for him to collect, though he'd managed to get the few organs he could still recognize into specimen bags, which were now tucked into one of his repurposed aluminum tackle boxes, stacked next to the carcass beneath the tarp that covered the truck's bed.

He hadn't intended to cart his current mutilation into Denver to pick up his wife, but as with any vocation, sometimes life got in the way. If he had gone to the veterinary labs at the university before heading out to get Tammy, she would have been stuck at her work for an extra few hours, and she'd been at the office since 5:00 a.m. already. If he'd delayed getting her that long, she would have cut off his head and put it in the back of the truck next to the cow's.

He knew he was playing with fire, pushing her close to a breaking point. She was already working crazy hours at the packing plant to cover most of their household bills and keep them and the kids in healthcare, while he'd been cutting back his freelance hours at the microchip firm to focus on his investigations. Even worse, in the weeks since the Duran mission, he'd had to ramp up his equipment expenses, spending hundreds of dollars on better field tools, and to retrofit his specimen and storage facilities. He'd done his best to cover up exactly how much he'd been spending on his new equipment, but Tammy had always been good with numbers, and ever since she'd been bringing in the lion's share of the home income, she'd been in charge of the credit cards and bank accounts.

They'd somehow managed to keep any out-and-out fighting to a minimum. She'd exploded on him only twice—once when he'd maxed out the MasterCard on a laboratory-grade organ freezer the same afternoon she'd tried to make a payment on their youngest son's braces; the second time when he'd spent three hundred dollars at a pawn shop for a set of scalpels that would have made Jack the Ripper blush, the morning after their washing machine had a seizure, spitting soap bubbles all over the basement of their house. But lately, even her silent stares had the feel of liquid nitrogen.

But Chuck couldn't pull back. He knew he was getting closer to *something*. To him, Duran had been a true turning point.

The fact that Star Team status had been pulled from the mission had ended up working in Chuck's favor. Because of the lack of funding from Bigelow and MUFON, he'd been forced to find his own means to study the samples he'd collected from that streambed and the nearby ground anomaly.

For the scarred soil, he'd turned to a private soil analysis lab, the same lab that performed studies for Colorado State's agricultural department. At first, the lab had given him pushback when they'd realized the nature of his investigations, but as long as he assured them that their lab name wasn't posted on his blog or given to any media contacts, they were willing to run studies on his samples at limited cost. Though the soil he'd collected at the ground anomaly didn't test markedly different than soil from a different part of the field where the cow had been found, there had been a difference in what the lab called "exchange capacity" or solubility. For whatever reason, the soil within the anomaly was far less soluble than that in the rest of the field.

Chuck had no way of interpreting the finding, so he'd shifted his attention to the bio samples. Through cold calling and the sort of conversational magic he was known for, he'd made a connection at the Colorado State College of Veterinary Medicine and Biomedical Sciences, in Fort Collins, just two hours from his home in Colorado Springs. One of the top veterinary pathologists at the college, a Dr. Colleen Duncan, DVM, had been intrigued enough by the cattle mutilation coverage she'd seen in the local news to agree to see his samples. When he'd quickly driven over to the college, he'd found her to be an amiable skeptic; she wasn't a believer, but she was interested enough in his work to take seriously whatever he could bring her.

She'd led him on a tour of her lab and then had looked over his samples.

Almost immediately, she'd given him the bad news that the storage of the bio samples was insufficient. The isopropyl alcohol and water mix recommended to Chuck had contaminated the specimens, voiding any type of blood analysis, and the containers they had suggested had caused out-gassing. Still, under a microscope, Duncan had been able to see that there had been no hemorrhaging in the Duran cow, meaning the animal had been dead before it had been mutilated. There was no indication of any laser cau-terization, but the cuts were precise and sure, which was disconcerting.

Although the Duran cow itself wasn't going to provide Chuck with any new insights into mutilations, it instantly opened up a relationship that had helped his work. Shortly after he'd taken in the Duran samples, Dr. Duncan had invited him back to give a presentation to her students at the veterinary school on cattle mutilations. After the presentation, he was offered the opportunity to sit in on a horse necropsy. Through the necropsy, he learned exactly what he'd need to bring the vets for a more conclusive study: an animal dead within twenty-four hours, without any obvious signs of natural demise, predator death, or poisoning.

Within days, he'd found a calf that fit the criteria, a mutilated animal void of blood that had died mysteriously on a ranch in Trinidad County.

From the start of the necropsy, the vet realized she was seeing some-thing she'd never seen before. The animal's heart had collapsed, telling her that the blood had been drained. There were no signs of blood pool-ing in the carcass, leading the vet to assume that the animal had bled out, but when she was shown photos of the area around the mutilation site, and had seen that there was no blood on the ground or anywhere in the vicinity, she was left with no easy answers. Where had the blood gone?

And then she had worked her way into the animal's mouth—to the missing tongue. Chuck would never forget the sight of her wide eyes above that surgical mask.

In the car with his wife, Chuck said, "Tammy, I'm really on to some-thing here. These animal mutilations aren't going to be explained away. This isn't going to end with some mocked-up picture of a weather bal-loon. Something real is happening out here, and I might be the only one who can figure it out."

Tammy's face didn't change, but he could still feel that liquid nitrogen in the air between them.

"You get so sure about these things. You get so excited and you're just so damn willing to believe. It scares me, how far you're willing to go. It's so clear to you, but don't you wonder—maybe it's just, well, you."

"This isn't some little piece of metal from an old debris site," Chuck said. "It's—"

"No, it's a dead cow rotting away in the back of our truck."

Chuck reached across the seat between them and yanked open the glove compartment. A thick file, bulging against a rubber band, slid out onto her lap.

Tammy looked at him, then undid the rubber band and started to leaf through the pages. Slowly at first, then faster, moving from the photos to the brief notations, from the lab postings to the names and dates. He could tell that a part of her wanted to remain unaffected, another part wanted to look away, but both were impossible. Seeing it laid out like that, page after page:

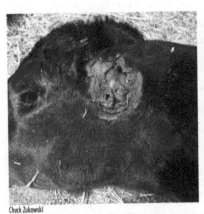

Chuck Zukowski    Chuck Zukowski

*Both ears left and right side cut out in a circular fashion . . .*
*Oval hole where ear used to be*

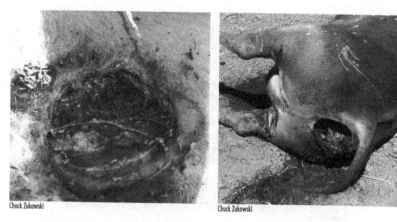

*Oval hole at udder, teats cored out . . .*

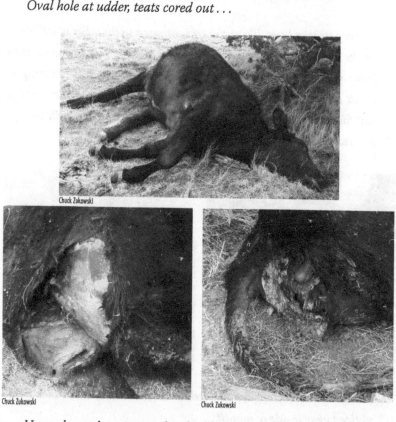

*Upon closer observation, they had been surgically removed.*

Manuel A. Sanchez

*... very strange laser-like cut marks common to the other mutilations in the area, but latest mutilations have taken a very dramatic turn from what he's witnessed before. Rather than the laser-like cutting on adult animals, the attacks are now on calves. And not one, but he's lost four within 3 weeks. All four were not just merely mutilated but basically destroyed ...*

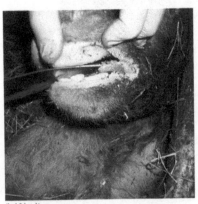

Chuck Zukowski

Chuck Zukowski

*Mouth open and tongue removed, small amount of dried blood was noticed near inside of mouth.*

Chuck Zukowski

Chuck Zukowski

*Left side of face was removed, approximately 48 square inches of flesh missing. The blood markings on the snow to the left of the wound are from me rolling the animal over to get a better look at it.*

*. . . we discovered a bizarre and unnatural sight. The brain and ear of the cow appeared to have been removed (through surgical methods . . .) . . .*

Chuck Zukowski

Chuck Zukowski

*Circular incision on right side including the ear. Some hide is seen where the upper ear used to be.*

*Picture of mouth showing little damage and lack of a tongue . . .*

Tammy didn't reach the last page. She closed the folder against her knees, shook her head. Her eyes looked watery, but Chuck didn't know if it was because of the images she had just seen, the stiff breeze coming through her window, the dead meat smell in the car—or because of him.

"But why does it have to be you?" she asked. "Why does it have to be in the back of our goddamn truck?"

"Couldn't be helped," Chuck said. "You called when I was just leaving the ranch. Dr. Duncan—"

"Dr. Duncan doesn't believe in UFOs."

Chuck lowered his voice.

"I think she believes more now than she ever did before."

After the last body he'd brought in, Duncan had admitted that there was no clinical explanation for what Chuck had been finding out on those ranches. And yet a lack of an explanation wasn't proof. To the skeptics, it was the opposite of proof.

*So close.* To Tammy, to people unwilling to believe, he seemed as far away as he had always been, but Chuck knew better. He knew there was a connection between these mutilations, and that this phenomenon was part of something enormous—even if the mainstream world was still willing to ignore them. And it wasn't just the mutilations themselves; it was their proximity to UFO sightings. Numerous ranchers had seen unmarked helicopters before and after finding their livestock's remains. There were other stories like the one from Dulce, New Mexico, where a single ranch had lost fifty cattle, where an investigation had shown evidence of some sort of craft having landed nearby, and where there'd been multiple eyewitness accounts of multiple choppers. Something big was going on, and had been for decades. *Military? Alien?*

"I know this is hard," Chuck started, and then he paused.

His eyes had drifted to the rearview mirror again. The flatbed truck had shifted to the other lane, giving him an unobstructed view back down the highway. Maybe one hundred, two hundred yards back, he saw what looked to be a black SUV. He couldn't be sure—the sun was now down far enough that the sky had turned a dull gray, the headlights flashing brighter, glare bleeding through to the edges of his vision. But it could have been a black SUV.

His hands tightened on the steering wheel. It didn't mean anything, he told himself, plenty of people had black SUVs. Plenty of people took the highway from Denver to Colorado Springs.

Except, it wasn't the first time he'd seen an SUV like that, or the second, or the third. Just a few weeks earlier, at one of the ranches he'd visited, he'd even seen one parked on the side of the road not two miles down from where he'd been cutting away at a freshly mutilated cow. The SUV had been empty, no driver, no passengers, nobody, and Chuck had even pulled over, gotten out to check the plates. He'd considered running them through the computers at the sheriff's department, but had realized that would have been an illegal crossing of a line that he wasn't yet willing to cross.

Hell, it was probably nothing. And even if it wasn't, he couldn't be sure who they were. Or why they might want to be keeping tabs on him.

On the blogs dedicated to MUFON, the current theories about Bigelow and the Star Team program were that Bigelow was using the information it was getting for the program to conduct its own investigations, sending out teams ahead of the MUFON field agents to gather whatever evidence might be available. Shadowing, people called it, though Chuck thought shadowing was exactly the wrong word. Shadows came after something, not before.

If it was true, it was a fairly brilliant plan. While considering UFO reports for Star Team status, Bigelow had access to information on sites before anyone else. If some sort of evidence was out there, they'd be in the perfect position to get there first. Still, one had to wonder, what, exactly, were they searching for? Or what, exactly, had they already found?

Chuck moved his eyes to the road, then back to the mirror, back to the car that might have been an SUV, now drifting farther back, three hundred yards.

Were they Bigelow investigators, interested in what he was finding out on those ranches? Was it someone else—the CIA, the government, the military? Or was anyone following him at all?

Tammy's head was back out the window again, the folder tightly closed against her lap. He still hadn't mentioned anything to her about the sense that he was being followed, shadowed, whatever. Either she would have thought that he was crazy, that his obsession now included paranoia, that he needed help, or she would have believed him, which might very well have been worse. They had kids, a family, neighbors who held barbecues on the Fourth of July. She would probably have asked him—told him—to stop.

But Chuck couldn't stop, not now. If there really were people shadowing him, it was just more proof that he was getting close to some answers.

# CHAPTER 26

## SCAMMON, KANSAS,
## APRIL 8, 2009

**37.2783° N, 94.8211° W**

*Hyperspace, baby.*

Three in the morning, maybe closer to four, tires clinging to a stretch of razor-straight Kansas highway. Seventy, eighty, ninety miles an hour, the bright-red 2005 jeep's headlights lit up the snow, a flickering vortex of white rising, then splintering into horizontal sheets against the ice-caked windshield.

Debbie Zukowski grinned like a maniac as she put more pressure on the pedal, her body hunched forward over the steering wheel. She knew she was driving way too fast for the conditions; it had been snowing since she'd left the baseball game—because of a call in the seventh goddamn inning, Cardinals' opening day. She had two hundred miles behind her, but the adrenaline spiking through her veins was too hard to control. She had been waiting for a call like this, and even one on opening day—her personal Vatican—hadn't dampened her enthusiasm.

When she'd gotten the call to deploy, she'd paused only long enough to make one phone call to her brother before heading to her jeep. To her surprise, Chuck had been almost as excited as she was; his own frustrating experience with his Star Team false start hadn't stopped him from being proud of his big sister: A Zukowski was going to head the first official MUFON/Bigelow Star Team investigation after all. Chuck's only advice to her, as she'd checked the equipment she kept in the jeep's trunk and consulted the MUFON files that had led to the Star Team designation, was to take it slow and careful.

He should have known better. If Chuck was excitable and enthusiastic, Debbie was a fracking Tasmanian devil. For days, she had been frantically lobbying the MUFON brass about the files that were now spread out across the passenger seat to her right, barging into a half dozen directors' meetings at the Kansas City headquarters, demanding that someone get out there into the field, pronto, before evidence disappeared. She'd fully expected to get the case, but she hadn't guessed that Bigelow would be interested enough to foot the bill.

Their acceptance and then rejection of Chuck's Duran cattle mutilation had been much discussed in the Kansas City offices; to be fair, Bigelow and MUFON were still figuring out the parameters of their relationship. Debbie was a big girl; she understood: Falling in love was one thing, making a marriage work was quite another. Judging from Bigelow's history—and his current aerospace company—he wasn't interested in chopped-up cows. He was after flying saucers.

And that's exactly what Debbie had brought him. In return, she was going to be the first official Star Team investigator, funded to hit the field running.

*At hyperspeed.*

Her smile widened as she peered through the snow. From her maps, she was getting close, which meant she needed to keep her eyes open— one errant blink and she was going to blow right past the place.

According to her files, Scammon, Kansas, was a little fleck of nothing of a town, an eight-block village with one Mexican restaurant, a single fire engine, a nearby sheriff's office, and a population of 832, attached to the rest of the country by three train tracks and a single highway. Scammon held fields, corn, snow, wind, cold, and a lot of nice country people, including one middle-aged woman with two sons, seventeen and fourteen. This woman had just recently seen and reported a house-sized UFO.

Debbie had talked to the woman twice already, first when her report had come into MUFON's website, then again when she'd gotten the notice to deploy. She hadn't been surprised when the woman had answered the phone in the middle of the night; considering what she'd reported seeing just two days earlier, it was unlikely that she'd been getting much sleep since. Although she'd gotten over her initial wariness of Debbie—who was part of a national organization with offices in numerous states, even if it had no official ties to the government or military—she seemed thrilled that someone was finally going to listen to her, in person. She'd quickly agreed to a face-to-face—now just a few hours away.

Chuck had been surprised that Debbie was going to be running the investigation on her own; he'd even offered to fly down from Colorado Springs in the morning, to help her out. But though Debbie enjoyed their joint investigations, she knew Chuck's feelings about MUFON. Even though his analyzing expertise at animal mutilations had brought him enormous respect throughout the organization—there was already talk of making him a director in charge of investigating the mutilation phenomenon—he was obviously more comfortable working independently. This was going to be a MUFON/Bigelow show.

In the initial deployment call, Debbie had been told to expect to be met by a pair of Bigelow agents in Scammon and that she would probably recognize them by sight, because they'd be wearing white shirts and dark suits. To her, it seemed like a strange sartorial decision, feeding right into the general suspicions of the UFO crowd—the clichéd Men in Black, who would no doubt stand out in small-town Kansas as brightly as the

UFOs they were chasing. But she was comforted by the fact that they'd be bringing gifts: more equipment, paid for by Bigelow, and a check for her expenses, as well as a fifty-dollar per diem.

So she was on her own, but not entirely alone. And on top of Bigelow's men, she'd have her brother on speed dial. He'd promised to lock himself in his office for the duration of her investigation, so he could be on standby in case she needed his advice. *Charlie to her angel.*

She laughed out loud, heading faster into the snow. Maybe that was the best way to work with a talker like her little brother. Keep him a disembodied voice on the other end of a phone.

If he got annoying, she could always hang up.

.  .  .

The house was exactly what she had expected, boxy and white, with a triangular roof and a screened-in porch, embraced on either side by a well-kept yard, at the end of a rural stretch of road at the edge of town. She'd gone through Main Street, past a lovely spired church, to get there, and the woman who'd met her at the door could have walked right out of a quilting catalogue.

She'd even offered a glass of lemonade, which Debbie had dutifully accepted. The beads of condensation running down the sides of the goblet-sized vessel were now painting rings on the cover of Debbie's MUFON file, which she'd left closed on the coffee table between them. Even though she'd basically memorized the damn thing in the few hours between reaching Scammon, checking into her motel, and arriving at the woman's house, she wanted to hear it again in the woman's voice. This was the UFO business, after all: First contact was always preferable to words on a page.

"It was after 1:00 a.m.,"* the woman said, her subdued tone signaling

---

* Dialogue from report submitted to MUFON, via http://www.ufo-hunters.com/sightings/.

that she was still shaken by the event, days later. "My seventeen-year-old and I were driving out to look for my other son. He'd gone missing after school—forgot to tell me he'd gone over to a friend's garage to work on his car, but I didn't know that then—and we were heading east, toward the train tracks."

"The train tracks?"

"See, there's no gate on them, just three tracks running right past the town. Mother of two boys, you got to worry about things like that. Anyway, we were heading east, and then we just saw it. Huge, bright orange, just above the trees to the north. It wasn't round or square or oval—I couldn't tell what shape it was, it was just so bright."

Debbie leaned toward her, nodding.

"You say huge . . ."

"And I mean it. Big as a house. At first I believed we were being bombed, but then I saw that it was going up, not down. My son starts screaming, 'What is that?' So we turned north and followed it."

"You followed it?"

The woman had a fierce look on her face.

"Hell, yes. My son is screaming at me to call the sheriff, but I knew they'd think we were nuts. My son grabs my cell phone, takes a picture of the thing . . ."

"You've got the picture?"

Debbie had seen the photo in the file, but that didn't keep her pulse from rocketing as the woman scrolled to the image and handed over her cell phone. It wasn't much to look at—black background, orange light. They weren't photographers, but a woman and her kid in a moving car. Still, it was something. *Category 2, at the least.*

"Doesn't look anywhere near as big in the picture. Best way I can express it—it was like a big mobile home in the sky."

Debbie could picture Chuck's smile at the description. Insight into what the mainstream media thought of people who believed in UFOs.

"Then the thing just disappeared. I was freaked out, I drove back to our house. We were sitting in the driveway when it came back. My son yells 'Go after it,' but as soon as we pulled out, it flew out toward the edge of town, was blocked by the trees, then vanished."

Debbie whistled low.

"Hell of a thing," she said. "Did anyone else see it?"

"Hard to say. About five minutes later, a sheriff's patrol drove by. Either someone called him, or he had seen it himself."

A police car usually meant a police report, even in a small town like this.

"And your kid? He made it home safe and sound?"

"Gave him hell, too, had me thinking he'd been yanked up into that thing. Better than getting run over by the train, but not by much. They yank you up—they don't put you back down the same, do they? At least that's what I've heard."

Debbie had a dozen MUFON files that agreed, but her own experience with abduction cases was limited. Chuck could probably have told the woman stories that would have scared her into locking her kids in the basement for the foreseeable future.

Debbie reached for her file.

"I'm going to follow up on a few things, and I'll get back to you with whatever I find."

"Your people," the woman said. "They ever actually find anything? I mean, anything solid, anything real? Or is it just a lot of searching."

Debbie paused for a sip of the lemonade. She wasn't sure how to respond.

"Mostly it's searching. Getting reports like yours, following up in the field, again and again and again."

Then she finished with the lemonade, grabbed her file, and turned toward the door.

"Thing is, the job might be mostly searching. But you only have to actually find something once."

• • •

Debbie had never been good at waiting. Even as a kid, she'd been the type you didn't want to leave too long in a waiting room, whether the dentist's office, the pediatrician's, or even the school principal's, because there was a good chance that given enough time, something was going to get broken. She wasn't destructive by nature, but her threshold for disrespect was set a bit lower than most people's. And to her, that's what it meant to be put on hold in a room filled with uncomfortable chairs and a nonfunctioning water cooler; it was a signal that she was low on the totem pole.

It seemed doubly disrespectful to be kept waiting for over an hour at the local Scammon, Kansas, sheriff's office, a building so nondescript that Debbie had driven by it twice before she'd pulled into the parking lot off Main Street. She could tell by the look on the receptionist's face—a mix of desperation-level boredom and glazed defeat—that there wasn't much else going on to occupy the tiny police force's time. But even so, there she was, counting the unnerving dust particles she could see floating within the oddly yellow-tinged water cooler, waiting for someone to come out of the closed door behind reception, to at least acknowledge her existence.

She was considering what damage she could do—though she was a little scared of what the liquid in the water cooler might do to her MUFON-issued boots, and the chairs in the waiting room seemed heavy enough to withstand a fair tossing—when a police officer finally came out of the back room, and headed toward her with a look that almost rivaled his secretary's.

Tall, a bit pudgy, with enough gray hairs above his wrinkled forehead to tell her he'd been in Scammon long enough to know everyone twice, he shook her hand as she rose from her seat, then raised an eyebrow to tell her to ask whatever it was she needed to ask. So she got right to the point.

"I'm looking for a police report from two nights ago," she said, partly fishing. "An officer was dispatched around one-thirty in the morning."

"She means the sky lighter," the receptionist suddenly butted in, the look on the woman's face shifting toward something resembling life, if not enthusiasm. "Orange thing. Big as a house."

The police officer still had his hand out, midshake. He looked at the receptionist, then at Debbie. And without a word, he let go of her hand and headed for the door.

Debbie stood there, shocked. The officer never looked back; he simply opened the door, stepped outside, and was gone. Debbie turned to the receptionist, who simply shrugged.

"Can you get me a copy of that report?" Debbie tried.

The woman shrugged again.

"Sorry, there's no report."

"When an officer's dispatched . . ."

"Sorry, really can't help you. There isn't any report from that night."

"But the sky lighter," Debbie said, using the woman's own words.

"Big as a house, I heard."

"But there's no report."

The woman tapped her fingers against her desk, then shrugged for a third time.

For a brief moment, Debbie tried to guess how heavy the water cooler was, and how hard it would have been to toss the thing over the woman's desk. *Probably easier than it would be for Chuck to bail her out of a Scammon jail cell.*

"Thanks for your help," she said, and headed out the same way the officer had just gone. Of course, he wasn't outside; she could see his police car pulling out of the parking lot, mere feet from where she'd parked her red jeep. She couldn't be sure, but she thought the officer paused long enough to read her license plate before exiting onto Main Street.

Curious, she thought to herself. And then she reached for her cell phone.

• • •

Three hours later, she was still talking to Chuck as she pulled into the parking area of her motel. To her surprise, the lot wasn't empty, as it had been when she'd first checked in that morning. One other car was parked right up next to where her room was situated. The car was black, big— and had government plates.

"I don't like this," Chuck brayed in her ear as she pulled up next to the car. The windows were tinted, but by squinting she could see that there was no one inside.

"Could be a coincidence," she said.

"In a town like that?" Chuck said. "And after what went down at the sheriff's office? No way. I think you should take off."

"I'm not going anywhere. I haven't checked out the tree line yet— where the UFO disappeared. According to my maps, there's a field right around there, back behind a farmer's house. Maybe there's a ground anomaly."

"And maybe there's a military detachment cleaning up a debris field."

Debbie thought for a moment. She understood Chuck's concern. He'd told her about his belief that strange vehicles had been shadowing him for some time, but neither of them could say for sure that it was anything beyond paranoia, which came with the territory with this kind of work. You stayed up late reading about UFOs and military cover-ups, you started to see things behind every rock and tree. Then again, a parked car with government plates was not a trick of the mind. And many conspiracies were very real. Hell, she herself was supposed to have been met in Scammon by two men from an aerospace company with FAA and NASA ties that built pieces for the International Space Station; a company that had been funding UFO studies for more than a decade, and was now financing a MUFON UFO response program.

"Look, Chuck, I left opening day in the middle of the seventh inning.

I'm not going home because a small-town cop gave me the run-around and there's a fed parked at my motel."

She put the jeep into reverse and headed back out of the parking lot.

It took twenty minutes to find the farmhouse and another three before Debbie realized the location was going to be another dead end. The man who answered the door—denim overalls, baseball hat, a radio blasting some sort of evangelical talk show in the background—told her he hadn't seen anything out back, wasn't the owner of the farm, and she wasn't welcome snooping around in the field behind the house. And when he finally slammed the door in her face, she turned around to see a pickup truck blocking her jeep in the driveway.

She'd taken two steps toward the truck when it suddenly went into reverse, fast enough for the tires to spit plumes of dirt into the air. Then it was gone down the highway.

Debbie's stomach was doing flips as she got back behind the wheel of the jeep and pulled out after it. She wasn't giving chase—she was simply trying to work out what was going on in her head—but she hadn't made it fifty feet down the two-lane highway when she saw the pickup truck coming toward her in the other lane.

It slowed as it passed her. Just like the government car in the motel parking lot, the windows of the truck were tinted. And the way the sun was now high in the sky above her, Debbie couldn't see past the glare bouncing off the glass to get a look at the driver.

As the truck shrank in her rearview mirror, she contemplated pulling a U-turn; but before she could, she saw four more cars coming toward her in the other lane, three of them black SUVS, one a dark blue sedan. They passed one after another without slowing, but she had no problem seeing the vehicles' plates. All of them had federal designations.

"What the hell?"

She waited a minute for them to shrink like the pickup, then dialed Chuck as she made the U-turn.

She was hanging a good distance back—but could still see the last of the caravan—when Chuck answered, and she quickly explained what was going on.

"Debbie, get the hell out of there. Come back with a team or find your Bigelow contacts."

Debbie kept her foot steady on the pedal, making sure she didn't get any closer to the last car.

"Hell, for all we know some of these guys *are* Bigelow. And if I leave now, you know what will happen. I'll come back tomorrow and it will be like nothing ever happened."

"So what are you going to do? Follow them up and down the highway until they arrest you?"

"For what? Anyway, it doesn't look like I'll have to follow them very far."

The caravan of cars had made it to what passed as the town's outer limit and was pulling off the highway into the parking lot of a Mexican restaurant, a flat, ranch-style building with cantina lights strung around the windows. As Debbie drew closer, she counted even more cars parked out front of the entrance. Some of them were unmarked like the SUVs and the truck, others were cop cars, county and state. She was pretty sure she also saw the officer's car from earlier that day, though the cop who'd ignored her at the sheriff's office was evidently already inside the restaurant.

"Something is going down here."

She slowed, waiting for the drivers of the caravan she had been following to exit their vehicles and head inside. When the parking lot seemed quiet, she pulled in after them, choosing a spot as far back as she could. Then she turned off her jeep.

"Chuck, what do you think?"

Chuck was quiet on the other end. Obviously, he was still scared for her, but his curiosity had to be jumping as high as hers. Local cops, Kansas cops, feds—it was something neither of them had ever seen before.

"Public restaurant," Chuck said. His own curiosity had obviously gotten him past his fears.

"Tacos and enchiladas, according to the Internet. Good margaritas, but it's barely noon."

Chuck paused a moment.

"You could always use a cup of coffee."

Debbie grinned. Then she ran a hand through her hair, making sure the golden curls ran all the way down to her shoulders, and got out of the jeep.

When she reached the front door, she was pleased to discover it was unlocked. Then she stepped inside and found herself facing the main dining area. Orange ceiling lights, porcelain-tiled floor, a long bar decorated with plastic chili peppers, and in the center of the room, a wide, rectangular table surrounded by chairs. At least twenty people were seated in those chairs, mostly men, but at least two women, some of them in suits and ties, a few in police uniform. The officer from earlier in the day was seated directly across from where she was standing, his attention on the man at the front of the table, who was obviously in charge and holding open a file. Half out of his seat, the man wore obvious FBI-black pants, white shirt, and black shoes. A walkie-talkie was chirping at his belt.

Someone at the table coughed and then everyone looked at her. The officer from earlier had a shocked expression, eyes wide beneath his salt-and-pepper hair. Debbie smiled at him and waved.

"Hi, Sheriff."

The FBI agent at the head of the table slapped the file down and pointed toward the door.

"Restaurant is closed."

Debbie didn't turn around. She flipped her hair, trying to look as blonde as possible.

"Oh, that's okay. I just want a cup of coffee, won't take but a moment."

"I said, the restaurant is closed."

"Then I'll just use the bathroom and be on my way."

The police officer rose halfway out of his seat.

"The bathroom is closed, too, ma'am."

Debbie knew she had pushed it as far as she could. She flipped her hair again, then headed for the door.

"My mistake. I'll find the next one."

She was breathing hard as the door swung shut behind her. Her feet barely touched pavement as she raced for her jeep. Her heart was racing, her fingers trembling against the steering wheel, but she managed to get the jeep out of the parking lot and back on the highway before she dialed Chuck again.

"Time to go," she said. "I don't know what this is, but it isn't normal."

Her jeep was moving fast down the highway—seventy, eighty—but when she looked in the rearview mirror, she easily saw the pickup truck, and right behind it, one of the SUVs.

"Crap."

"They're following you?"

"Looks like it. Although there's only one way in and out of this town, so it could be a coincidence."

"Yeah, right. If they pull you over . . ."

"I'll keep you on the phone the whole time."

Debbie could feel the sweat running down her back as she kept the car right at the speed limit. She did her best to keep her eyes on the road in front of her, but every few minutes she couldn't help looking in the mirror: pickup, SUV. Not close enough to truly scare her, but always there, hanging fifty yards back, matching her speed.

For the first few hours of the drive, her heart was in her throat, her thoughts racing. But by the time she'd reached the Kansas border, she was more surprised and curious than scared. She'd gone through a few minor traffic jams, made a couple of quick turns—and still, there they were, hanging back behind her, keeping pace.

The strange parade continued like that for the entire six-hour drive. When she was about three miles from her house, stopped at a red light, the pickup truck finally shifted closer, getting to less than a car length back. The truck revved its engine once—then honked. The driver's window rolled down and a man leaned one arm out and waved at her.

Then the truck pulled a sudden U-turn, blocking traffic from the other direction. The SUV followed suit, tires skidding against the pavement. Then the two vehicles were gone.

Debbie's heart pounded in her chest. Someone sure as hell had just sent her a message. Her investigation into whatever had happened in Scammon, Kansas, was over. If they were willing to follow her for six hours, to within three miles of her house . . .

The light in front of her turned green, but she just sat there, breathing hard.

# CHAPTER 27

## RUSH, COLORADO,
## AUGUST 12, 2010

Chuck was ten yards out of the corral when he spotted the television camera—so strangely out of place, propped up on a shiny metal tripod sunk a few inches into the muddy embankment that led down to the highway where Chuck had left his truck, buglike lens staring out over the ranch like some sort of miniature, invading Martian from the old pulp version of *War of the Worlds*.

The cameraman stood a few feet from the tripod, in deep conversation with a woman who couldn't have been anything other than a television reporter. Pretty, from her chiseled, porcelain features to her perfectly sprayed, honey-colored hair, she was wearing a suit that had no place on a ranch and shoes that made even less sense. Beyond them, Chuck could make out the TV van parked close to his own vehicle. Satellite dish on top, the local Fox logo emblazoned across one side.

Even though Chuck had been expecting the reporting crew, he still felt a wave of discomfort as he led Glenda toward the waiting camera. No matter how many animal mutilation investigations he had conducted since Duran, there was still something about them that felt personal and private. He was a pioneer in a field few people understood or even acknowledged, and it was hard not to be suspicious of anyone from the outside, looking in. At the same time, he knew the importance of getting the story of this phenomenon out to the public.

Lately, he'd been making every effort he could to draw attention to his work. Although Tammy would have called it counterintuitive, he believed that the more people who knew who he was and what he was doing, the less dangerous his work became. Especially after what had happened with his sister in Kansas, being tailed by what appeared to have been government cars, it no longer felt safe to be operating quietly and independently. In Chuck's mind, it was better to be mocked in public than to feel threatened in private. Then again, Debbie wore the perceived threats as a badge of honor; to her, the Scammon investigation had been a success, even though she hadn't been able to get any further than an interview with a witness to a UFO event. She was certain something significant had happened in Scammon, and Bigelow had agreed enough to cut her a check, for the first Star Team mission—even though no Bigelow agents had ever attempted to make contact. If Bigelow's people had indeed been on the scene, they had been conducting their own investigation, either parallel, or in MUFON's place. For Chuck, it was just more evidence that the aerospace company was working a much different agenda than Debbie was willing to admit. Chuck believed it was no longer enough to be careful—it was important to be paranoid as well.

But a TV van wasn't an uninvited SUV, and a reporter with high cheekbones and too much hair spray wasn't an agent from a mysterious Nevada aerospace company.

When the producers at Fox had called Glenda a short time after Koen's piece for a second interview, she'd told them that she'd cooperate only if Chuck was investigating. Chuck had been honored, if not surprised, by her willingness to trust him. He understood ranchers, and over the past year, they had come to trust him. Since Duran, he had been to dozens of mutilation sites and had spent many hours with his veterinary experts at the university. He had even rewritten the MUFON handbook on mutilations using the information he had learned and was now considered MUFON's top expert on the phenomenon.

Chuck agreed to the Fox interview, not because he needed more personal affirmation or because he liked being on TV, but because he knew that the more he became the public face of the phenomenon, the more likely it was he'd get the call when the next mutilation happened. That meant getting to the scene faster, and a better chance of finding real evidence. *Undeniable, smoking-gun, physical evidence*—in his mind, he'd already uncovered plenty of evidence, from the metallic fragment at Roswell to numerous carcasses drained of blood to detailed witness accounts. But to the rest of the world, to his wife, none of that was enough. He needed that UFO landing on the White House lawn.

As he closed in on the camera crew, the female reporter broke away from the cameraman and started toward him. Glenda touched the back of his arm, leaning close to his ear.

"Not sure how much I like these people on my ranch, Chuck."

"I hear you. But I think we owe it to Princess and Buck to get the story out there."

Glenda let go of his arm as the reporter gave them both a smile that was blinding and white, bright enough to cauterize a scar.

## 7:15 P.M., TWO DAYS LATER

Chuck's spine felt as if it was collapsing onto itself as he hunched against the stool in his kitchen, staring at the small TV on the counter by the sink. Tammy was next to him, holding his hand, but he could barely feel her fingers. The TV screen had shifted to a commercial, some damn, colorful splash of idiocy involving tampons or Viagra or dishwashing detergent, but Chuck's mind was swirling backward to the short report he had just watched, the five-minute segment that would quite possibly shatter his life.

Tammy spoke first.

"This isn't right," she said. "That woman lied. Chuck, she lied."

"Could have been a mistake," Chuck finally managed.

"She sounded so certain. But she was talking out of her ass."

Tammy grabbed a folder from the top of a pile on the stool to Chuck's left and angrily flipped it open. The police report was right on the top, faxed and photocopied, but perfunctory and perfectly legible. Signed and officiated by the two officers who had first arrived at the mutilation site in Rush when Glenda had first reported the incident. Tammy ran her finger down past the details of the case—the cost of the dead horses, the strange wounds the officers had found, the bizarre lack of blood or signs of struggle—to the official police conclusion.

"Animal cruelty. The police report couldn't be more clear."

Chuck continued staring at the screen. He knew the police report by heart, he knew what he had seen at the ranch—and he remembered exactly what he'd said in the interview, because he'd just watched it, as it aired, minutes ago. His words had been slightly different—"animal mutilation"—but they were accurate, and did not contradict, in any way, the official police investigation.

Had the Fox report simply ended with him on the Rush ranch, everything would have been fine. But instead, they'd continued the report with an interview with a PR woman from the sheriff's department—worse yet, placing the two interviews side by side. And despite the file beneath Tammy's finger, the PR woman had offered a completely different official statement:

"Predator cause," Chuck repeated the woman's words, which still reverberated in his head. "A mistake, a lie, I don't know. She's clearly misinforming the public."

Was she told to lie by someone at the department who didn't want to create a panic about the strange phenomenon taking place on the nearby ranches? Or had she simply not read the report, assuming, like most skeptics, that a mutilated animal on a ranch had to be the work of predators?

"Maybe it won't matter," Chuck said, but he didn't believe the words himself. He knew what the report was going to look like. Even though he'd been so careful over the years not to mention his affiliation with the sheriff's department during his investigations, even though he'd never worn his uniform and had done his best to keep church and state separate, the way the report had been set up, he was contradicting his own department.

"Maybe this will just blow over," he said.

Tammy slapped the report down on the stool next to him. As upset as he was, he felt buoyed by her anger. They'd been battling for so long about his growing obsession with his investigations, he'd assumed this would be the final straw—that he'd let an animal mutilation interfere with his work as a deputy, that he'd gone on TV and gone public in a way that would bring attention to their family. And yet here she was, completely supportive, on fire with anger. She didn't need to believe in what he was doing. She believed in him.

That knowledge alone was worth more than anything the department could take away from him.

•  •  •

A gun, a badge, shined to perfection, glowing in the light streaming through the kitchen window, and the department patches from his uniform, laid out next to each other on the cutlery island he'd installed eight months earlier, reparation to his wife for that UVF reader he'd bought from a Denver pawn shop.

One week later, Chuck and Tammy were back in the same place they had watched the Fox report—except now Chuck was standing, arms stiff behind his back, as he watched two uniformed police officers trying to navigate their way around his fury of a wife.

"He served for a decade. Putting his life at risk every time he put on that uniform and for no compensation. What gives you the right?"

Chuck wanted to stop her, but he didn't have the energy. Even though he'd mentally prepared himself for the moment, had prepared all the equipment the department had requested for retrieval, it hadn't actually hit him until the lead officer, a Sergeant Waters, had apologized for what he was about to do, when Chuck had first let him into the house.

It wasn't until that moment that it had actually set in: They were there to take his badge. He was no longer going to be a sheriff's deputy. A thousand memories went through his head and then he no longer had the energy to be angry, just disappointed.

After the Fox newscast, he had been called into a meeting at the department, where he'd been confronted by one of his commanders. The man accused Chuck of representing the sheriff's department while running UFO investigations. Chuck argued back that he'd never mentioned his affiliation or worn his uniform during his UFO work. The only "evidence" they'd found was that, on a website bio, he'd mentioned his reserve status. But the officer hadn't cared.

The real reason they were after him was that he'd contradicted their PR flack by stating the truth: Those horses on the Rush ranch hadn't been mutilated and killed by any known animal or predator. And Chuck was in a position to know that, better than anyone else.

"He's done everything you've asked for ten years," Tammy shouted, still between the officers and the cutlery island, "and this is how you treat him? Because of a ridiculous TV report?"

"Tammy," Chuck said.

"No, this isn't right. They shouldn't be allowed to do this."

But she finally stepped aside. The sergeant quickly swept the gun, badge, and patches into a satchel and handed the equipment to the other officer. Then he gave Chuck a look, mostly consoling, but with a touch of what Chuck interpreted to be derision.

And Chuck understood. That was how this worked. He'd learned it from years of investigations, from reading everything that had been written about Roswell, mutilations, and others like himself. You didn't need a conspiracy to hide the facts that people like Chuck were trying to uncover, because nobody could even investigate those facts without facing ridicule, and worse. Pilots and army officers couldn't report UFO sightings without risking their careers. Scientists couldn't study strange phenomena without risking their academic posts, enduring mockery, laughter, and scorn. Journalists couldn't cover even the most obvious of incidents without their work being compared to science fiction.

And a reserve sheriff's deputy and part-time microchip engineer couldn't try to draw attention to a mystery that affected thousands of people without risking everything he loved.

He was glad his kids were out of the house, Ashley, especially, because she had always been so willing to believe. He couldn't bear to imagine what she might have thought, watching the officers take his badge simply for trying to find answers. No matter what she might have felt inside, Chuck was certain she would have told him to keep searching. She would have demanded he keep going, keep being that UFO nut, because deep down, that's who he was.

# CHAPTER 28

## COLORADO SPRINGS,
## AUGUST 23, 2011

One-thirty in the morning. Eyes open.

Pupils dilating, the physical a fraction of a second ahead of the subconscious. Black shifting to gray as little slivers of moonlight slipped through the cracks in the blinds covering Chuck's bedroom windows. The barest particles of light refracting through cones and rods, blurred shapes and shadows solidifying into solid objects: dresser drawers, closet doors, bookshelves, bedposts.

And then Chuck was rising quickly out of the bed, doing his best not to wake Tammy as he extricated himself from the complex twists of double sheets and duvet covers. Tammy liked a comfortable bed, and lately it had felt like it was the least Chuck could offer her. God knew the money wasn't coming fast and furious from the few hours a day he worked in microchips, and now that the rest of his time was entirely focused on the outer-worldly, their conversations had become painfully one-sided. As a cop, he'd been forced to keep grounded on a day-to-day basis, dealing with the public, navigating departmental bullshit, the tragedies and thrills and sometimes terrors of the details he was sent on. Tammy had understood those gigs and communicated with him about them. But now, sometimes he was so far off the ground, he might as well have been one of the UFOs he was chasing.

But thoughts like these, which had dominated Chuck's life a year ago in the weeks and months after they had taken his badge, were far from his mind as he hit the floor of his bedroom with bare feet and moved quickly toward the hallway that led to his office. It was the second time in two consecutive nights that Chuck had found himself jolted awake. The night before, the cause had been instantly clear: At 11:46 p.m., his bed had been moving. Lurching and shaking beneath him, jerking up and down hard enough to wake even Tammy, engulfed in her cloud of overstuffed linen. The shaking had lasted only ten or fifteen seconds, but it had been palpable enough to throw books from the bookshelf onto the hardwood floor and to knock over two plastic action figures from the last *Star Wars* movie that had somehow migrated from his office to one of the bedroom windowsills.

The power had gone out, but it had taken Chuck less than ten minutes on his ham radio—another in the long list of fundamental tools of his trade that kept Tammy in two jobs while he carved out hours up in the mountains, out in the forests, down the desolate highways—to find out that they'd just experienced a 5.3 earthquake centered nine miles outside Trinidad, Colorado. Although it hadn't killed anyone or caused extensive damage, the Colorado earthquake had been rare enough to end up in newspapers across the country. The *New York Times* had called it the "largest natural earthquake" in the state in more than a century. Had Chuck still been a deputy, he would have found himself responding to dozens of calls from terrified neighbors.

Instead, he'd added a pin to the map on the wall of his office—bright green, signifying a natural geological disturbance, in contrast to the mauve pins signaling the many shallow quakes tied to fracking, a more and more frequent phenomenon in the area—and gone back to bed.

But now, a night later, it wasn't a quake moving the bed beneath him that

was sending him rushing to his office. It was the thought of another earthquake fifteen hundred miles away. A 5.8-magnitude quake centered in Lou-
isa County, Virginia, one of the strongest in Virginia's history, had occurred
earlier that afternoon, fifteen hours after the quake that had hit Colorado.

Chuck reached his office, pausing long enough to quietly shut the
door behind him. Although he knew Tammy wasn't going to follow him
inside, especially the way things had been going over the past year, he
needed to make sure he was alone. Because the thoughts that were running through his head were crazy enough on their own. The thought of
sharing them with someone else . . .

He flicked on the lights to his office and slowly approached the enormous map hanging from the wall.

There were so many pins now, of so many different colors, that the
thin, glossy material looked bowed in the middle. The contours of the
United States were plumped out by the pull of gravity and so many
marked anomalies that the map looked a little like one of his investigations, like a carcass that had been sitting at the edge of a stream too long.
And yet it wasn't the entirety of the map that possessed Chuck, at that
moment, it wasn't the rainbow of pushpins or what they represented. It
was just two of those pins—bright green, fifteen hundred miles apart.

Chuck stood there, back to the closed door, shifting his gaze from
one of those pushpins to the other. Virginia, to Trinidad, Colorado, and
back again.

Even without the weight of all Chuck's anomalies and investigations,
the map was drawn with a slight curve—an attempt at projecting, in two
dimensions, the area's true geographical parameters, taking into account
the curvature of the Earth and the oblong nature of the north-south axis.
Because of this, it wasn't instantly obvious from a casual glance, but as
Chuck focused back and forth between the two green pins, it became
clear: The two earthquakes had occurred fifteen hours apart, more than
fifteen hundred miles apart, along the same parallel.

This wasn't the revelation that had jarred Chuck awake for the second night in a row: In fact, he'd noticed the odd coincidence earlier that day, while at his desk at the microchip company he was currently freelancing for. After reading about the Virginia quake that afternoon, he'd pulled up an app on his phone that recorded earthquake data from around the world and had taken note of the data. The Colorado quake had occurred along the Sangre de Cristo fault line, with coordinates of 37.0412° N, 104.4726782° W. Meaning the disturbance had occurred along the 37th parallel—a fixed geographical location based on a point's distance from the equator, the horizontal "center" of the mostly spherical Earth. Each "imaginary" latitude line was exactly parallel to the equator, measured in perfect increments from the North Pole, at 90° North, to the South, at 90° South.

The Virginia quake, it turned out, had been due to a tectonic shift at the Central Virginia Seismic Zone, at the coordinates 37.557787° N, 77.554492° W.

Again, on the 37th parallel.

Two earthquakes, both the strongest in years occurring on the same parallel, separated by fifteen hundred miles.

Chuck considered himself a scientist. He spent his work hours as an engineer, and his investigative time attempting to apply scientific methods and equipment to phenomena most usually described as paranormal. He knew that two data points like the two quakes meant nothing; they were most likely a meaningless coincidence. Millions of earthquakes a year occurred all over the world, and many of them had to be occurring on the same parallels. That was simple statistics. And besides, he wasn't a seismologist. There were plenty of conspiracy theory links between seismological events and paranormal phenomena, but that wasn't Chuck's focus.

What had torn through Chuck's mind and woken him up was something that occurred to him, subconsciously, when he'd been placing those pins earlier in the day.

Over the past year, since the events at the Rush ranch and his subsequent firing from the sheriff's department, Chuck had thrown himself headfirst into his investigations, mostly focusing on animal mutilations, adding in the odd UFO sighting that reached his attention. Although he'd lost much of his access to the reports that came through the police department or via other officers, his firing had actually caused his public profile to get bigger. Andy Koen and his local TV affiliate reported on Chuck's unceremonious expulsion from the force, and that had been carried by multiple media outfits, making headlines across the state. The reports hadn't always been kind—being fired from the sheriff's department for investigating cattle mutilations and for studying UFOs was controversial enough on its own, without the department's continued insistence that he'd been fired for contradicting them in public, not for being the Mulder of El Paso. But either way, the notoriety had given him the publicity he'd needed to step up his investigations—and to begin getting to anomaly sites faster than ever before.

Hard evidence still eluded him, but over the past year, he'd kept his veterinary associates at the university busy with almost-fresh carcasses, and he'd been adding mostly confirmed, unexplained mutilations to his map at a geometric rate.

So many data points, so many colored pins. Looking at them, he could see past the plastic and the punctured map, beyond the imprint behind the glossy material to the spot where his daughter's Mickey Mouse poster had once happily hung, beyond his house to those ranches where he'd stood, sometimes knee-deep in mud, looking down at a murdered, bloodless cow or horse. He could smell the death in the air, could hear the ranchers' heavy breaths as they contemplated such brutality. So many data points, like stars in the unobstructed Colorado sky. More than twenty years of data, his life's work, his obsession, the only thing that could possibly have ever come between him and his wife, a random swirl of color and carcasses and unexplained, unimaginable chaos.

And yet, there was something more. Chuck was suddenly sure of it.

Without really thinking, he reached forward and began pulling off pins. Not at random—he pulled only the pins that were unconfirmed sightings or mutilations, the pins signifying reports that had yet to be studied, calls that had come in through his sister at MUFON or through his own sources or due to his own muted celebrity. Reports that hadn't been investigated, that might very well have been pranks or hoaxes or mistaken identities—airplanes flying where they weren't supposed to, navy missile launches, crop dusters, actual weather balloons.

He kept pulling pins, leaving only the unexplained mutilations or UFO sightings he himself had studied, or that had been confirmed via history, MUFON, or his sister. He kept pulling pins, until suddenly, he stopped and stepped back.

To his utter shock, he saw something quite spectacular:

A surprising majority of the animal mutilations and UFO sightings bunched along one geographical band, spanning across the midsection of the map. Where the scientist in Chuck would have expected a random distribution of events, what he was looking at was a mathematically significant pattern.

Chuck stared. And then he reached forward and began furiously yanking all the pins from the map. The Rush horse mutilation that had gotten him fired from the sheriff's department. The mutilation at Duran, his aborted Star Team excursion. The Taos Hum, which had been documented by so many over so long a period. The Mantell UFO sightings in Kentucky. Mutilation after mutilation, anomaly after anomaly, UFO sighting after sighting. He pulled all the pins until the map was bare, its glossy surface broken only by a rolling sea of tiny puncture marks.

He turned to his filing cabinets, pulling open drawer after drawer, retrieving folder after folder, piling them on the desk, the floor, every open surface, until he was standing in a sea of folders.

Chuck Zukowski

And then he began again, from scratch, putting the pins back into the map. Working from his files, he started with his recent mutilations:

| Duran | 03-08-09 | 37.121634° N, 104.777872° W |
|---|---|---|
| Sanchez | 11-17-09 | 37.07.373° N, 105.18.549° W |
| Sanchez | 05-17-11 | 37.11.476° N, 104.18.718° W |
| Miller | 08-08-11 | 37.16.940° N, 104.18.718° W |
| Miller | 03-17-09 | 37.16.443° N, 104.21.10° W |
| Crested Butte | 08-20-10 | 38.860763°N, 106.998038° W |
| Aaron | 12-12-09 | 3706.246° N, 105.21.475° W |
| Garren | 03-22-09 | 37.31.915° N, 10430.003° W |
| San Luis | 11-09-10 | 37.152219° N, 105.404844° W |

Moving deeper into his files, he worked through his own UFO investigations and on to the numerous files that Debbie had sent him from MUFON's records, again focusing only on the coordinates of events that could be corroborated by multiple witnesses, or that had enough circumstantial evidence for him to consider them verified:

| ~37.733742° N, 97.344318° W | El Pueblo, KS | blue |
|---|---|---|
| ~37.8265933° N, 96.8618466° W | El Dorado, KS | blue |
| ~37.6859933° N, 95.4580888° W | Chanute, KS | blue |
| ~37.6552346° N, 98.734834° W | Pratt, KS | blue |
| ~37.97426° N, 100.872108° W | Garden City, KS | blue |
| ~37.1775639° N, 113.684729° W | Ivins, UT | orange |
| ~37.1153943° N, 113.5811668° W | St George, UT | orange |
| ~37.142123° N, 113.506463° W | Washington, UT | orange |

| | | |
|---|---|---|
| ~37.5213989° N, 112.7882762° W | Cedar City, UT | orange |
| ~37.6539191° N, 84.7717229° W | Danville, KY | purple |
| ~37.4830076° N, 82.5197184° W | Pikeville, KY | purple |
| ~37.0876458° N, 88.6020655° W | Paducah, KY | purple |
| ~37.1021135° N, 88.079959° W | Paducah, KY | purple |
| ~37.00257° N, 86.4433923° W| | Bowling Green, KY | purple |
| ~37.1719792° N, 87.6929031° W | Dawson Springs, KY | |
| ~37.99399° N, 85.7180113° W | Shepherdsville, KY | |
| ~37.3152755° N, 89.5164931° W | Cape Girardeau MO, | |
| ~37.1472169° N, 92.769157° W | Seymour, MO | |
| ~37.5999419° N, 90.6277523° W | Ironton, MO | |
| ~37.5616009° N, 90.2943544° W | Fredericktown, MO | |
| ~37.3606262° N, 90.6978259° W | Annapolis, MO | |
| ~37.6163512° N, 93.411915° W | Bolivar, MO | |
| ~37.5616009° N, 90.2943544° W | Fredericktown, MO | |
| ~37.3606262° N, 90.6978259° W | Annapolis, MO | |
| ~37.6163512° N, 93.411915° W | Bolivar, MO | |
| ~37.6204875° N, 93.4119854° W | Bolivar, MO | |
| ~37.968525° N, 90.0544183° W | St Genevieve, MO | |
| ~37.2669576° N, 90.1197865° W | Grassy, MO | |
| ~37.7387343° N, 92.8589877° W | Bennett Springs, MO | |
| ~37.1558012° N, 90.6957447° W | Piedmont, MO | |

| | | |
|---|---|---|
| ~37.0043354° N, 91.9645091° W | Willow Springs, MO | |
| ~37.649247° N, 93.0911549° W | Buffalo, MO | |
| ~37.3100726° N, 89.9701676° W | Marble Hill, MO | |
| ~37.9675273° N, 92.9683002° W | Mack's Creek, MO | |
| ~37.2209224° N, 93.2917786° W | Springfield, MO | |
| ~37.6964509° N, 90.6398177° W | Iron Mountain, MO | |
| ~37.7788665° N, 122.4198916° W | San Jose, CA | |
| ~37.6317274° N, 120.9925405° W | Modesto, CA | |
| ~37.247656° N, 80.002376° W | Roanoke, VA | |
| ~37.4496867° N, 79.1452602° W | Lynchburg, VA | |
| ~37.2652577° N, 107.8804513° W | Durango, CO | |
| ~37.169055° N, 104.4992543° W | Trinadad, CO | |
| ~37.343534° N, 108.625789° W | Cortez, CO | |
| ~37.9967524, 105.696512° W | Valley View Hot Springs, CO | |
| ~37.1219185° N, 104.7777849° W | | |
| ~37.121634° N, 104.777872° W | | |
| ~37.1242559° N, 105.2791322° W | | |
| ~37 07.373° N, 105 18.549° W | | |
| ~37.1029625° N, 105.3573559° W | | |
| ~37 06.246° N, 105 21.475° W | | |
| ~37.1916244° N, 105.4601859° W | | |
| ~37 11.476° N, 105 27.406° W | | |

| | | |
|---|---|---|
| ~37.2812758° N, 104.3061755° W | | |
| ~37 16.940° N, 104 18.718° W | | |
| ~37.5300546° N, 104.5369699° W | | |
| ~37 31.915° N, 104 30.003° W | | |
| ~37.1524422° N, 105.4046469° W | | |
| ~37.152219° N, 105.404844° W | | |
| ~37.2696425° N, 104.3473846° W | | |
| ~37 16.443° N, 104 21.10° W | | |

The more pins he added, the more frantic he became, almost manic. He knew what he must look like. But already, the map in front of him was beginning to tell its impossible story again. He hadn't even scratched the surface of his own files—let alone the thousands of other sightings that he and Debbie and even MUFON didn't have access to, from around the country and around the world. But even so, the image on the wall was impossible to ignore. Eventually, he intended to recheck all the coordinates using freely available NASA or Google satellite imaging and transfer his findings onto his computer, but he was certain the digital image would be no less vivid:

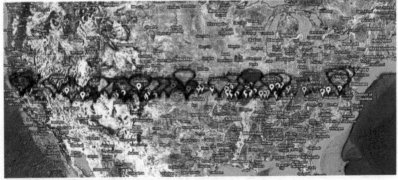

Chuck Zukowski

Chuck knew that the human mind was built to seek out patterns and that much smarter men than he had driven themselves crazy chasing symmetries that seemed to make sense in the dead of night, but were nothing more than shapes and shadows in the bright light of day. But where the mind could play tricks, numbers were anchors into the real world. Numbers, math, science, these were the tools of the skeptical—and the numbers were telling him that he'd stumbled onto something mind-blowing.

Standing there, staring at the map, he realized he needed help; maybe not the sort of "help" Tammy might have only semijokingly suggested, but help from a like mind.

He reached across to his desk and found his cell phone, then snapped a picture of the map and put the photo into a text.

Less than three minutes later, his office was filled with the first few bars of the *X-Files* theme song, as his phone began to ring.

• • •

"What the hell am I looking at?"

Debbie sounded surprisingly awake for four-thirty in the morning. Chuck hadn't been surprised that her phone ringer had been on that late into the night. She was one of the top field agents at MUFON, after all, and UFO reports tended to come at night, but usually she ignored him just long enough to piss him off. Then again, the photo wasn't something so easy to disregard.

"I'm still trying to decide what to call it. The Paranormal Highway has a nice ring to it, doesn't it? Or maybe the 37th latitude, or parallel. Let it be more of a mystery, because hell, that's what it is, isn't it?"

The 37th parallel wasn't entirely accurate. Although many, if not most of the phenomena seemed to have occurred on the geographical 37th latitude, a number were closer to the 36th or 38th. Chuck liked the mental image of a highway extending between the 38th and 36th parallels that encompassed the majority of anomalies.

"These pins . . ."

"Cattle mutilations, UFO sightings, most of your MUFON reports. I focused only on the reports I could reasonably verify or had studied myself. It's only partially complete. But I think it's still pretty impressive."

"No kidding."

Debbie was quiet on the other end for a moment. Then Chuck could make out the rustling of papers in the background; she'd obviously shifted to her own home office, which was similar to his own, minus a few dozen plastic alien toys.

"Funny thing, Chuck. We've been looking into a couple of big cattle mutilations here in Missouri, one in Norwood, one in Piedmont. I'm checking for the coordinates on them—yes, both on the 37th."

"Pretty strange, isn't it?"

"Joplin Spook Lights, Missouri, 37.090514. The Mantell Incident, Owensboro, Kentucky, 37.7737. The incident in Irvington, Kentucky, 37.881967, 86.284218. Aztec, New Mexico, 36.830447. Cape Girardeau, Missouri, 37.313656. Taos. Quite a highway."

"The only big hitter that's missing is Roswell," Chuck said. "Roswell is on the 33rd. But you know, when you think about the connection between Roswell and the original flying saucer reports made by Kenneth Arnold near Mount Rainier, just a few days before the Roswell crash, well, anything moving from Rainier to Roswell would have to pass right through our highway."

Maybe he was grasping to add a data point. One more anomaly that fit or didn't wasn't going to change whatever it was they were looking at; if every latitude could be imagined as some sort of highway running horizontally across the country, it appeared that the 37th was the most traveled by the sort of anomalies the two of them had dedicated their lives to studying.

"I think we can take this further," Debbie said. "When Bigelow's NIDS was looking into the Big Black Deltas, the first thing they did was try to link the sightings with known or unknown military bases. If we take the same tack, I think we're going to find a few more interesting data points. Because looking at your map, I'm pretty sure Area 51 is on the 37th. And so is NORAD, at Cheyenne."

"The Pentagon is on the 38th," Chuck said. He was already back into his files. Searching for more military bases, he also found himself noticing other landmarks with a connection that might be relevant—American Indian sites, both sacred and historic. Most tribes had their own unique mythologies involving the outer-worldly—he wondered if there might be some reason for so many of their important sites to be linked to this same paranormal highway. Either way, he was already adding more pins to his map:

| | |
|---|---|
| The Pentagon, Arlington, Virginia | 38.871523 ° N, 77.055963° W |
| Fort Knox, Kentucky | 37.909534° N, 85.946045° W |
| Area 51, Nevada | 37.6150857° N, 115.8593802° W |
| Cheyenne Mountain Nuclear Base | 38.7425° N, 104.8484° W |
| Mammoth Cave National Park, Kentucky | 37.193416° N, 86.102312° W |
| Zion National Park, Utah | 37.195331° N, 112.983398° W |
| Canyonlands National Park, Moab, Utah | 38.32442° N, 109.89624° W |
| Monument Valley Navajo Tribal Park, Utah/Arizona | 36.998166° N, 110.110474° W |
| Navajo State Park, Arboles, Colorado | 37.006939° N, 107.430688° W |
| Comanche National Grassland, Pritchett, Colorado | 37.186579° N, 102.930908° W |
| Cimarron National Grassland, Elkhart, Kansas | 37.015712° N, 101.815796° W |
| Chaco Culture National Historical Park, New Mexico | 36.071302° N, 107.969019° W |
| Ancient Bristlecone Pine Forest, Big Pine, California | 37.182202° N, 118.306274° W |

| Land's End Labyrinth, San Francisco, California | 37.780314° N, 122.511642° W |
|---|---|
| Cahokia Mounds, Illinois | 38.656292° N, 90.059323° W (Native American site) |

Chuck Zukowski

"Am I just going crazy?" he said, into the phone. "Or is this something?"

"I don't think the sentiments are mutually exclusive. Some of this has got to be coincidence. Some of it is probably related to the reporting mechanisms. Where we're situated is informing the kind of reports we see, and the ones we can verify. But even with all of that—I wouldn't expect this much of a correlation."

Chuck agreed. There was clearly a pattern here: A highway of anomalies spreading from one end of the country to the other, along the 37th parallel.

"What do you want to do with this?" Debbie said. "Put out a press release?"

There was no humor in her voice—she knew Chuck had always believed in publicizing everything he'd found, as early as possible.

"If you're wrong, if this is nothing but coincidence, paranoia, insanity, you'll look like an idiot. If you're right—that might be worse."

He guessed where Debbie's thoughts had gone. Scammon, Kansas. Chuck could see the pin right there on his map, 37.2783, right along the 37th parallel.

He didn't need to go to Kansas to face his own fears. Hell, he wondered what he'd see, parked along the curb, if he pulled back that window shade on the other side of his office.

"I need to dig deeper, continue investigating. But where do I even begin?"

"I think you began more than twenty years ago."

She was right. Without realizing it, he had been studying incidents along this paranormal highway for most of his life. Two decades of UFO sightings and animal mutilations, scattered along a geographical line that had also, apparently, been the latitude of choice for government bases and American Indian holy sites.

What he'd uncovered was the bare beginning of something—there were many directions he could go from where he stood. Using his training as a deputy, he thought: What made the 37th unique, what might link all these sites, these anomalies? Magnetic properties. Astronomical connections. Solar, lunar, wind, geology.

He could spend his life searching for an answer.

Hell, he *would* spend his life searching for an answer. Animal mutilations, UFO sightings, military bases—all gathered along a geographical line running down the center of the country. Somehow, there had to be a connection.

Running his finger along the map, he found himself pausing over a clump of colored pins.

"I can think of at least one natural starting point. From Area 51, through my mutilations and sightings in Colorado, past the Taos Hum. The first significant cluster of phenomena—cattle mutilations, UFO sightings, supposed underground military base, even Skinwalkers . . ."

"Dulce," Debbie said.

Dulce, the Archuleta Mesa, Ute Mountains. The location encompassed the Gomez ranch, where more than fifty cattle had been mutilated, leading to an investigation that had found evidence of some sort of flying craft in the vicinity, as well as witness reports of unmarked helicopters—considered a sign of military interest, if not involvement. The Gomez mutilations that had led the New Mexico senator to push for a federal investigation. Likewise, the high frequency of incidents—mutilations, UFO reports, Skinwalkers—had caught the interest of Bigelow's NIDS organization. Bigelow had sent some of the same scientists he'd embedded in Skinwalker Ranch in Utah to investigate Dulce. If Bigelow believed Dulce was worth real scientific analysis, it was a good place for Chuck to start.

In fact, Chuck realized, he had already started with Dulce nearly a decade ago.

Without warning Debbie, he placed his cell phone down on the corner of his desk and dug back into his files, pushing through pile after pile until he found the correct folder. He paused briefly on the photos—Kodaks, mostly, old enough that the color was bleeding in some places, mostly of his kids and Tammy, a couple from inside the RV, only one or two of the mountain range itself and the nearby backside of the Archuleta Ridge. But he didn't need photos to remember the strange, bright lights in the sky, or that scream from the elk, or whatever it might have been, that had died, gone silent, so suddenly.

Not Dulce, exactly, but very close—right up in the great Sleeping Ute Mountain, so named because it was supposed to resemble a Ute tribal chief, supine and slumbering. The same Ute tribe whose mythology Bigelow's people had gotten to know so well at Skinwalker, the same mountain range that supposedly harbored an underground base that many believed was connected to something anomalous.

Chuck had once taken his family in his RV to that spot right smack along the 37th parallel, a place he'd been drawn to by an email from a psychic, a place he believed he'd seen a UFO.

Back then, he'd been such a novice, such a hobbyist. He'd been so careful—with his kids and wife at the nearby motel waiting for him, he hadn't gone any deeper down the MUFON category scale than a moderately close contact. He'd seen the lights in the sky and had heard the animal go down, but he hadn't followed the noise down the tree line, he hadn't looked for the place where whatever had happened, happened.

He looked up from the file, toward the map on the wall.

His kids were mostly grown up. He was an expert in animal mutilations and UFOlogy. He'd been playing an odd cat-and-mouse game with some sort of ever-watching organization, be it Bigelow, the government, god only knew. He'd lost his job as a sheriff's deputy, and was publicly known as a UFO nut.

This wasn't a hobby anymore.

He knew exactly where he needed to go. But first he had to present his theory to an audience much more intimidating than Debbie, who was born to believe. Before he headed back into the mountains, he had to take what he had discovered across the hall.

•  •  •

Halfway in, Chuck became flustered, lost, while trying to find the right language to make what he was saying sound anything but insane.

To his surprise, Tammy finally saved him from himself, interrupting him with the words he should have started with in the first place:

"So you believe there's some sort of UFO highway running along the 37th parallel?"

It was now a few minutes after five, and Tammy still looked half asleep, her hair in tangled twists above her head, a pillow still tucked under one arm as she stood next to him in the open doorway to his office. His presentation had started in the bedroom, but he'd quickly realized he wasn't going to get anywhere talking to a sea of sheets. If Tammy was going to understand, if she was going to at least listen, she needed to see it for herself.

And somehow, amazingly, she *had* seen it, and she hadn't yet run from the room screaming. That had to be a good sign.

"Coincidence?" she said.

"Maybe. Quite possibly."

After a long pause, Tammy finally spoke again.

"So where do we go from here?"

Chuck felt the smile move across his lips. He doubted she believed, any more than she'd ever believed.

But once again, she was willing to follow him down the rabbit hole.

# CHAPTER 29

## RUSH, COLORADO,
## AUGUST 15, 2011

*H*ell *of a thing to get past.*

Ten minutes before 11:00 a.m., and Glenda had her hands in the freshly turned dirt of the garden at the back of her ranch house, checking the moisture with practiced fingers as she eyed the tangle of weeds threatening the last row of carrots, right up by the irrigation joint. She'd have to take care of the weeds sooner rather than later, but she was taking her time—not entirely because of the heat, or the fact that she'd left the edged trowel on the porch, right next to Cody's new beanbag dog bed. She was procrastinating because for the first moment in as long as she could remember, things were finally beginning to feel normal again.

Over the past year, there had been good days and bad. In the beginning, it had mostly been the latter; she'd slept every night with the blinds wide open, Cody trembling and whining against her side. And she'd gone outside each morning expecting the worst; whenever she blinked, she'd see her poor horses lying on their sides in the dirt, torn and violated. She couldn't even think of them as Princess and Buck anymore, because that brought back too many memories, happy times she didn't want to link with the brutal images she couldn't erase from her mind.

Some of the reporters who'd come that first week—a trickle, then a drove as Chuck's firing led to a new round of interest from the local news stations—had asked her if she'd thought about selling the ranch, moving away. Usually, these were the reporters who'd made the trip from the big city, Denver, well-meaning, pretty people with Vaseline on their teeth and dye in their hair. Glenda had all but ignored their queries. She was a third-generation rancher. As traumatizing as the incident had been, leaving had never entered her thoughts.

But even so, she couldn't help wondering—what was it about her ranch that had brought her animals to such a violent end? Twenty-five head of cattle, a handful of horses; her neighbors to either side had much bigger ranches, much bigger herds. *Why Princess and Buck? Why her?*

Of course, it didn't do any good asking questions like that. There weren't any answers, not a year ago, not now. The only person who seemed capable of finding answers had raised only more questions, and had suffered for his efforts.

Glenda hated that Chuck had lost his position with the sheriff's department for trying to help her, but she couldn't say she was entirely surprised. She had always distrusted bureaucracies, and her experience with the local police had only bolstered her suspicions. Hell, the two officers who had first investigated the mutilations scene had come to conclusions similar to Chuck's—that the lack of footprints or struggle marks meant that whatever had killed her horses wasn't a common predator. And then, on TV, their PR representative had said the exact opposite, contradicting her own officers. After the fact, it had gotten even worse; when Glenda had spoken to the police investigators during a follow-up visit, they'd suddenly proposed yet another explanation—a lightning strike. Glenda had stared at the men in disbelief. Lightning had cut out her horses' tongues and left bloodless corpses behind?

Eventually, she had realized that outside help was a dead end. The police had been useless. Chuck was going to continue searching for the truth; he was one of the most determined people she had ever met, and he had more to prove than anyone. But for now, she was on her own.

Coming to terms with that fact had pushed her toward the normality she now felt, hands in the dirt as she contemplated a spaghetti tangle of common weeds, a wonderfully simple enemy compared to the unknown. Of course, normal was partly a state of mind; Cody still had those burn marks, and even a year later wouldn't go any farther than the front porch. King, the young horse who had witnessed whatever had happened to Princess and Buck, was a traumatized mess. Glenda feared that eventually, he'd have to be put down. And though she now closed the blinds when she slept, she still had those butterflies in her stomach each morning when she pulled them open, wondering what she was going to see.

But the dirt felt good in her fingers, and the sun was warm on the back of her neck. She even felt herself starting to smile as she brushed her hands clean against the knees of her jeans, rising to head back to the porch to retrieve the trowel.

She'd barely taken two steps when she heard Cody's whine rising above the warm breeze. Poor dog, she thought to herself. She had only theories—some improbable, some wild, some impossible—to recover from, but Cody had been there when it had happened, he'd seen it firsthand. But then she realized that Cody wasn't whining because of a memory.

Now she heard it, too—a dull thud coming from above, as much vibration as it was sound. Her eyes widened as she searched the sky over her ranch—and then she saw it, coming in low over the pasture behind her corral.

A helicopter. Unmarked, dark in color, maybe black, maybe a deep, unreflective green. The cockpit windows were tinted and opaque.

Glenda was frozen in place as the helicopter hovered over her pasture, directly above the spot where she had found Princess and Buck.

The helicopter circled twice, then began to rise. Higher, higher, then it banked hard to the left, speeding upward over her neighbor's ranch.

A moment later, it was gone, the low thud of its rotors receding into the wind. All that was left was the sound of Glenda's traumatized dog, still crying from her porch as he waited for her to return from the garden.

Glenda stood there, listening to Cody whine, for a long, long time.

# CHAPTER 30

Even ten years later, the memory of the animal's screams still echoed in Chuck's ears as he frantically made his way the last fifty yards toward the spot where he had calculated the elk, or whatever it was, had gone down, right beneath where he had once seen the strange bright lights dancing in the sky. Every step sent shock waves of fear through Chuck's body, but he refused to turn back. One hand was shakily holding his flashlight out in front of him, the cone of yellow light dancing across frozen brush and gravel. He didn't have his Glock with him this time, but instead a hunting rifle strapped across his back. Tammy had demanded he take the gun with him. Bears, cougars, she knew the sort of risks he was taking, going off alone into these mountains; she didn't need to see a map covered in colored pins to believe there was danger beyond that tree line. If he didn't check in within the next hour or so, she was going to be calling in park rangers from as far away as Dulce itself. Chuck hadn't told her that he doubted anyone, even rangers, was going to get permission from the local Native American tribes that controlled the area to come looking for him.

Chuck himself had needed to cut through an impressive amount of tribal tape to get himself back to the spot where he, along with his sometime assistant and the psychic, had first seen that UFO. Joe Fex had helped with some of that; a few contacts from Chuck's time at the sheriff's department had gotten him the rest of the way.

When he'd first finally arrived at the spot where he'd made camp ten years earlier, he had set up his equipment like before. His cameras, his infrared readers, his night vision. He'd then spent six hours sitting alone in the dark, watching the sky.

He hadn't seen any bright lights, he hadn't heard any animal screams. And yet he hadn't become disappointed, or frustrated, or numb; quite the opposite, he'd never felt more alive. This, too, was where he was supposed to be.

He'd been just about to break camp, a few brief hours before dawn, when he had suddenly felt something.

It was almost unnoticeable at first, more a stillness than anything truly palpable. And then a strange coldness had flickered through the air, a chill that hadn't been there before. When the breeze had finally kicked up again, it was tinged with something bitter and electric, something he had been able to actually taste on his tongue—as if some massive power line had just gone down. Chuck had assumed the EMF readings would have been off the charts, but he hadn't been willing to pause long enough to get the machine out of his pack. Nor had he expected that the battery in the damn thing would have been working if he had.

Instead, he had immediately rushed off in the direction he had remembered from a decade before—where that animal had gone down.

Animals dying, brutally, unnaturally—that was something he knew better than anyone in the world. That was what he had trained himself to understand.

Now, trampling through the thick trees, he let his adrenaline drive him forward; he knew that if he stopped to think about what he was doing, his fear would take over. He would have found himself racing back down the mountain.

Instead, he clambered over a jutting rock, pushed through a thick tangle of tree roots—and stopped dead.

████████████ was twenty feet in front of him, pitched forward ████████████ . Surprisingly compact, curved ████████████ metallic material ████████████ Roswell. ████████████ of incredibly high temperature; bones of what appeared to be half an elk lay on its side at the edge of the burned-out area, head turned up toward the sky.

Chuck stood frozen in place, his eyes shifting from the dead ████████████████████ was a noise, metal against metal, ████████████████████ reached up with both hands and twisted ████████████████ the thing in front of him wasn't an ████████████████████ . When Chuck looked more carefully, he saw the ████████████ .

Bigelow Aerospace.

████████████ Bigelow from ████████████ right path all along.

His 37th parallel was real—not a highway, but a *runway.* ████████ sightings, lights in the sky, Roswell, the animal mutilations, the Native American sacred grounds—████████████████ .

████████████ mankind ████████████ beyond.

Chuck had a choice; he could turn around and head back down that mountain, to where Tammy was waiting. Back to his life, and his research. As a CIA agent had once told him, he was not a threat, just another UFO nut, spouting nonsense on the Internet, part of a cottage industry of belief aimed at believers.

Or he could take that next step, and find out ████████████ open ████████ .

He could ride down that runway, wherever it might lead.

# BIBLIOGRAPHY

*Dulce Base: The Truth and Evidence from The Case Files of Gabe Valdez*, Greg Valdez. Levi-Cash Publishing, LLC, 2013.

*Hunt for the Skinwalker*, Colm A. Kelleher, Ph.D., and George Knapp. Paraview Pocket Books, 2005.

*Area 51: An Uncensored History of America's Top Secret Military Base*, Annie Jacobsen. Little Brown and Company, 2012.

*The Day After Roswell*, Col. Philip J Corso with William J Birnes. Pocket Books, 1997.

*The Roswell Legacy*, Jesse Marcel, Jr., and Linda Marcel. New Page Books, 2009.

"Investigation Casts Light on the Mysterious Flying Black Triangle," Leonard David. Space.com, August 5, 2002.

"Mr. B's Big Plan," Geoffrey Little. *Air & Space*, January 2008.

"The UFO Hunters—Scientists at National Institute for Discovery Science study anomalous phenomena," Brandon M. Mercer. Tech Live (TechTV).

"Mysteries of 'UFO ranch' in spotlight," Lezlee E. Whiting. For the *Deseret News*, April 22, 2006.

"UFO investigators reveal possible otherworldly relic," Cid Standifer. *Roswell Daily Record*, January 1, 2009.

FBI Records/FOIA, The Vault, Animal Mutilation.

"Why Do UFOs Love This Utah Ranch So Much?" Nina Strochlic. *Daily Beast*, July 2, 2015.

"Hotel Biz Zillionaire's Next Venture? Inflatable Space Pods," Vince Beiser. *Wired* magazine, October 23, 2007.

"Bigelow Aerospace shows off its vision for expandable space stations," Alan Boyle. NBCNews.com, March 13, 2015.

"A historical and physiological perspective of the Foo Fighters of World War II," Jeffrey A Lindell. 456Fis.org, February 10, 2014.

"In New Space Race, Enter the Entrepreneurs," Kenneth Chang. *New York Times*, June 7, 2010.

"Hypothesis; The Illinois Flying Triangle Is a Department of Defense, Not an ET Craft," NIDS. Las Vegas, Nevada, 2002.

"The Strange History of Robert Bigelow, Who Just Sold NASA Inflatable Space Station Modules," Ken Layne. TheAwl.com, January 17, 2013.

"Snippy the Horse, the most famous horse in the world!" Frank Duran. Snippy.com.

"Oregon MUFON Investigator's Guide," Keith Rowell. Paul.Rutgers.edu/~cwm /MUFON/field-investigators-manual.html.

Federal Government of the United States. Nevada Test Site Guide, DOE/NV-715, January 11, 1951.

# ACKNOWLEDGMENTS

First and foremost, I am indebted to Chuck Zukowski and his wife, Tammy, for opening up their lives to me over the year it took to pull this story together. Chuck is certainly one of a kind, and it was impossible not to be inspired by his enthusiasm about what he views as a quest for the ultimate truth, regardless of the consequences. I am also extremely thankful to Beau Flynn and Wendy Jacobson for introducing me to this story; I can't wait to see how it will look on the big screen.

I am immensely grateful to Leslie Meredith, my fantastic editor, as well as Donna Loffredo, Melanie Iglesias Perez, and the entire team at Atria/Simon & Schuster. I am also indebted to Eric Simonoff and Matthew Snyder, agents extraordinaire. I'm also thankful to the numerous named and unnamed sources who helped me put this story together—the experts, ranchers, and authors who blazed the trail I followed. And as always, I'm thankful to my parents, my brothers, and their families. And to Tonya, Asher, Arya, and Bugsy—all willing and ready to believe. I couldn't have done this without you.

# INDEX

# ABOUT THE AUTHOR

**BEN MEZRICH** graduated magna cum laude from Harvard. Since then he has published eighteen books, including the *New York Times* bestsellers *The Accidental Billionaires*, which was adapted into the Academy Award–winning film *The Social Network*, and *Bringing Down the House*, which has sold more than 1.5 million copies in twelve languages and became the basis for the Kevin Spacey hit movie *21*. He has also published the national bestsellers *Once Upon a Time in Russia*, *Ugly Americans*, *Rigged*, and *Busting Vega$*, and *Bringing Down the Mouse*, a book for young readers. He lives in Boston.